GHOST
ON
FIRE

Also by Michael Weller

PLAYS:
The Body Builders
Grant's Movie
Now There's Just The Three of Us
Tira Tells Everything There Is to Know About Herself
Moonchildren
Fishing
At Home (Split PART 1*)*
Abroad (Split PART 2*)*
Loose Ends
The Ballad of Soapy Smith
A Dopey Fairy Tale (in *Orchards*)

TRANSLATIONS:
Barbarians (M. Gorky)

GHOST
ON
FIRE

A PLAY

by *Michael Weller*

Grove Press
New York

Published by Grove Press, Inc.
920 Broadway
New York, N.Y. 10010

Library of Congress Cataloging-in-Publication Data

Weller, Michael, 1942–
Ghost on fire.
I. Title.
PS3573.E457G5   1987   812'.54   87-11957
ISBN 0-8021-3010-0 (pbk.)

Designed by Irving Perkins Assoc., Inc.
Manufactured in the United States of America
First Edition 1987

10 9 8 7 6 5 4 3 2 1

GHOST ON FIRE was first presented by the La Jolla Playhouse whose production opened on August 11, 1985 with the following cast:

DANIEL RITTMAN	Peter Zapp
LAUREL	Hannah Cox
NEIL TOOMIE	William Russ
JULIA RITTMAN	Helen Shaver
TOM COOPER	Timothy Shelton
ADEN PALTZ	Edward Zang
RALPH	James Hurdle
MICHELLE-MARIE TOOMIE	Holly Hunter
GINA	Kary Lynn Vail
AVRAM SCHENKER	Jan Triska
SYLVESTRE	Brett Weir
NATHAN BERGER	Bill Cobbs
NURSE	Kary Lynn Vail

Directed by Timothy Near

Sets by Thomas Lynch; Costumes by Jennifer von Mayrhauser; Lighting by Kent Dorsey; Music by Michael S. Roth and Holly Near

GHOST ON FIRE opened at the Goodman Theatre in Chicago on January 19, 1987 with the following cast:

DANIEL RITTMAN	Joe Guzaldo
LAUREL	Dawn Arnemann
NEIL TOOMIE	J. T. Walsh
JULIA RITTMAN	Celia Weston
TOM COOPER	Peter Aylward
ADEN PALTZ	Richard Fire
RALPH	Robert Langdon-Lloyd

MICHELLE-MARIE TOOMIE	Becky Gelke
GINA	Carol Huston Messing
AVRAM SCHENKER	Sidney Maryska
SYLVESTRE	Ron Crawford
NATHAN BERGER	Bill Cobbs
NURSE	Carol Huston Messing

Directed by Les Waters

Sets by Loren Sherman; Costumes by Martin Pakledinaz; Lighting by Stephen Strawbridge

CHARACTERS

DANIEL RITTMAN	a teacher, late 30s
LAUREL	a graduate student, early 20s
NEIL TOOMIE	a camera operator, late 30s
JULIA RITTMAN	Dan's wife, mid-30s
TOM COOPER	soap opera star, late 30s
RALPH	dissolute English doctor, 40s
ADEN PALTZ	philosopher, early 40s
MICHELLE-MARIE	Neil's wife, mid-20s
GINA	Avram's companion, 20s
AVRAM SCHENKER	Israeli millionaire, 40s
SYLVESTRE	ancient, frail butler
NATHAN BERGER	rural black man, mid-70s
NURSE	doubles with GINA

ACT ONE

DANIEL *speaks to us, smoking a cigarette.*

DAN: My name is Dan Rittman. I'm a teacher here in New York. Picture this: one morning we wake up to absolute devastation—buildings down, power out, crops dead on the stem, the Apocalypse, whatever. Overnight, we've been reduced to a savage world of kill or be killed, eat or be eaten . . . no diversions, no escape to the gym or the movies, no more fancy problems. Suddenly it's *right out there,* bold and simple and deadly. (*Beat.*) I have dreams about such a world, vivid dreams. I see my friends for the first time as they truly are: some cunning, some brave, some loyal and strong, others weak and treacherous, but always strikingly different from the way they appear in everyday waking life. And here's what's weird. Sometimes I stop and catch myself longing, desperately longing for such a world, like a great welcome burning away of all the lies and evasions. It's terrifying. I mean, why should I harbor such a deep desire to see the only world I know utterly annihilated? I'm an ordinary person, like you, alive in this most

1

pleasant of centuries, possibly the last, and like you, I want nothing more than to get through each day without hassles, doing as little harm as possible, minding my own business. (*Smiles.*) I have what I consider to be a highly civilized attitude towards life.

*   *   *

DAN's *office—desk, books, papers, movie cans, etc.* LAUREL, *a student, sits.* DAN, *script in hand, paces, then stops.*

LAUREL: I'm listening.

DAN: You're looking out the window.

LAUREL: And I'm listening, I can do both at once.

DAN: Would you like to schedule this some other time?

LAUREL: What other time? It's the end of the school year.

DAN: Fine. (*Beat.*) Alexis falls in love with Ken. Ken is an older man. He's married. Alexis knows this—

LAUREL: Meaning what?

DAN: I'm summarizing what you wrote.

LAUREL: I know what I wrote, I wrote it.

DAN: Laurel, the object of the exercise is to help you with your screenplay. You're welcome to reject everything I say, but as long as you're enrolled here and I am your advisor, you might as well listen. Students have actually been known to learn from this process.

LAUREL: Alexis falls in love with Ken. Ken is an older man. Alexis knows he's married. I'm listening.

DAN: Alexis and Ken have a fling—

LAUREL: A love affair. They *fall in love.*

DAN: They fall in love. (*Beat*.) But Ken won't leave his wife. Who by chance is flying to California on business. The plane crashes. She is killed. Ken is now free. But still he won't commit to Alexis. One day he tells her it's over—

LAUREL: And won't explain why.

DAN: Ken tells her good-bye. As he crosses the street, a car runs out of control and kills him. Alexis lays flowers on his grave. There are tears in her eyes. Fade. The End. Is that a fair synopsis of your story?

LAUREL: Yes, that is a fair synopsis of my story. So?

DAN: Don't you think it's just the tiniest bit arbitrary, killing off two of your main characters for no reason at all?

LAUREL: There's plenty of reason.

DAN: Yes, Alexis hurts, and she'd maybe like to see them both dead, but you aren't writing a spook movie about a girl with psychokinetic powers who makes people die when she doesn't get her way. It's a simple narrative about a love affair that doesn't work out, as many affairs tend not to, and that's what you have to show here.

LAUREL: It's my screenplay, I can do what I want with it.

DAN: Laurel . . . fiction has to reflect life, and life is never arbitrary; if you want to make stories, you have to find a unifying order beneath events so they unfold in a way that feels . . . well, true.

LAUREL: Okay. Then why *did* Ken leave Alexis? Tell me, Dan. After all the incredible times they had together? After he told her she was the only one he'd ever been able to really talk to? Why do you think he'd just call it off one day, no explanation, nothing?

DAN: I'm not here to write your screenplay.

LAUREL: How long are you going to pretend you don't know what this movie is about?

DAN: This is classroom time.

LAUREL: Why did you walk away? Don't I even deserve an explanation?

DAN (*beat*): Well, for one thing, my wife is not dead.

LAUREL: She would be if I had anything to do with it.

DAN: I assure you the feeling is mutual.

LAUREL: She knows?

DAN: That it happened, yes. Who it was, no.

LAUREL: So you talk to her but you won't talk to me.

DAN: There's no point, Laurel. Please.

LAUREL (*tries new tactic*): You've been daydreaming in class. They think maybe you're losing interest. I think it's something else that we could talk about.

DAN: No, Laurel, it's just me losing interest.

LAUREL: Oh, how smart and cool and above it all. Nothing gets to you, does it! Was I the first?

DAN: The first *what*? Affair? Student? Student this year?

LAUREL: You're such an incredible shit.

DAN: So you've been saved from a fate worse than death. And yes, you were the first in all three categories. Now, if you don't mind, I'd like to return to the thing I'm paid to do.

LAUREL: Oh fuck the script. It's stupid, I can't write, I can't do anything. I'm sick of this school. I'm getting out of here, don't worry—you won't have to put up with me next year.

DAN: Oh dear.

LAUREL: You find it amusing to watch your silly little fuckees go through their silly little agonies?

DAN: Listen to me! You show signs of real promise. You write excellent dialogue, believable, interesting characters. All in all, you're one of the most promising students I've ever had. Taught, sorry—*taught*.

LAUREL: What did I do wrong? No! I didn't say that. Fuck, I was going to be so grown up about all this, but it hurts, it just hurts. I miss you all the time.

DAN: Maybe we should assign you a different advisor next fall.

LAUREL: You're absurd, Dan. (*Laughs.*) You don't understand anything about anything, and you're supposed to be my teacher. What a laugh!

DAN: But I *am*, you see, I *am* your teacher, and that's the point, the only point. The two of us . . . it's absurd: starting over with someone who hasn't seen my ledger books. It's pointless, and irrelevant, and wrong, yes, just that, Laurel, it's *wrong*, because I had a responsibility to you, to the school, to my wife. You'll understand one day. Don't quit school. Please, for your own sake, don't do that.

> NEIL TOOMIE *peers around the office door. He wears mirror sunglasses, a Hawaiian shirt, and ankle-high Keds.*

NEIL: Greetings, peckerwood! Is major knowledge being exchanged here?

DAN (*beat*): Toomie?

NEIL: Don't let me interrupt. In fact, I'll join in, see if we can make a memorable event happen, all three of us—?

LAUREL (*rises abruptly*): Thank you for your help, Mr. Rittman. I'll try to make my story less arbitrary. Like life. (*Exits.*)

NEIL (*towards door*): Holy tamole, what a nubby little item. No wonder you teach. Well, Ritterfuck, ask me if it's good to be back.

DAN: What the hell are you doing here?

NEIL: Oh man, you are *so* New York, Danzer. All that head-on stuff. Ya already forget how we do it back in Hollyweird? "Hey, babe, you're looking good, been playing tennis, I like that tan"—you know, talk about how we look, admire the surfaces.

DAN: Unbelievable, you haven't changed a bit.

NEIL: Only more or less entirely, dickbrain, but how sharp of you not to notice. What brings me to the Big Macintosh? Movie of the Week for TV. A hard-hitting look at drug abuse. Or was it child abuse. I don't know, one of the "abuses." I haven't read the script yet, but the producer assures me it's gritty and real and uncompromising. In other words, another ninety minutes of prime-time toro poo-poo, yours truly behind the lens, Toom the Zoom, cameraman *extraordinaire*.

START

DAN: Yeah, I've noticed your name on a lot of TV stuff lately. I guess things are happening for you, huh?

NEIL *shows* DAN *a snapshot from his wallet.*

NEIL: My house. My yard. My swimming pool, of course. My illegal alien, Rosita the maid. My kids, Timmy,

Alec, and Jennifer, they speak perfect Spanish, get by in English.

DAN: Is there a wife in all this?

NEIL: Came with the house. Michelle-Marie. She'd be right about in there—what she calls the "viewing den."

DAN: Michelle-Marie? She's French?

NEIL: From the Bordeaux region of Texas. Met her on location, Taco Bell, express lane. Express romance, express marriage, express family, boom-boom-boom, three kids in five years. You know us Catholics.

DAN: Well, looks like you got yourself a life here.

NEIL: She's a good kid. Goes to church every week, puts up with me, God knows why, and He's dead so pick your reason. Mind like a prairie, Michelle: flat, endless expanse with one lone steer, grazing in the distance to symbolize *a thought!* (*Beat.*) So, this is where you spend your days now, eh?

DAN: This is where I spend *part* of my days.

NEIL (*smiles*): Ah, that old Talmudic accuracy, that fine-splitting of hairs, you dreadful Jew, you. How's Julia? Still the mad passion with you guys? She ever mention me?

DAN: Shit, I have to get to class. Listen, why don't we meet afterwards, grab a beer.

NEIL: Don't move a damn inch, scuzzbrain. I got a proposition you can't refuse.

DAN: We'll meet downstairs. An hour, tops.

NEIL: Gotta catch a train. Rhode Island. Visit the folks, you know. This'll only take a minute.

DAN: You have sixty seconds.

NEIL (*beat*): Hey, Danny, it's good to see your ugly face again.

DAN: Fifty-nine, fifty-eight, fifty-seven . . .

NEIL: All right, all right, I found us a backer.

DAN: For what?

NEIL: For what? For a film, asshole, what else is there? And he wants you to direct.

DAN: I'm not a director.

NEIL: Straight, man, this is money in the hand. Avram Schenker's his name, he's one of your tribe too, but the real McSchwartz: Israeli . . . fertilizer king of the Negev, made melons bloom in the desert, something like that. He's filthy rich, green as grass, and he's dying to break into film.

DAN: Cut the hustle. Israelis don't just wander out of the desert and throw money in your face.

NEIL: He saw some of our early work, student film festival, Haifa University, that's where he went. Get this—the guest speaker was François Truffaut, and he called our films the most original and deeply American work he'd seen in over a decade, quote unquote. Avram was impressed.

DAN: Neil, you're talking like fifteen, sixteen years ago we made that stuff. When was this festival?

NEIL: Avram's our age, so must be fifteen, sixteen years ago. Israelis have a long memory, what can I tell you. They're still ragged out over Palestine and that was what, two thousand years back?

DAN: Forget it, Neil. I haven't made a film in fifteen years.

NEIL: Like those three features don't qualify, the last one five years ago, I shot it, remember?

DAN: TV movies.

NEIL: That counts.

DAN: They were shit, Neil.

NEIL: But *classy* shit.

DAN: Shit is shit.

pause

NEIL: Okay, if you want to get technical.

DAN: Look, I appreciate your thinking of me. I do. But I'm a teacher now. It's taken me five years to put that other life behind, and I'm not about to upset the balance, not now. Not ever.

NEIL (*beat*): Okay, then just come with me for the weekend. *You're* the one he wants to meet. He's got this incredible estate in Maine, we'll blow some flake, do some jays, you tell him I'm hot, my script is dynamite . . . maybe he'll back me on my own. (*Beat.*) You owe me that much.

DAN (*pause*): What's the film, and make it quick, I'm already late for class.

NEIL: Ar-harr, first intelligent question of the day. Are you ready for this? Major mysterioso opening! Shot: highway, edge of industrial town, night, fleabag motel, one window lit, eerie music. (*Hums music.*) Slow zoom towards window. Cut inside: nervous balding guy with stethoscope. Girl on bed with legs up, trembling with fear. Shot: doctor's bag, hand reaches in, pulls out shiny chromium instrument—

(Neil)

DAN: Toomie, just tell me the fucking story.

NEIL: You're hooked, right! Just setting it up. Cut outside. A girl screams. Hold. Window slides open, doctor leans out, garbage can right under window sill. Doctor tosses in bundle wrapped with newspaper. Lid back on can, window shut, lights off inside. Music louder. (*Hums loudly.*) Suddenly the garbage can trembles. Lid slowly lifts . . . a tiny, unformed hand reaches out covered with specks of wet newspaper, music real loud now, head pops up—THE EMBRYO, IT'S ALIVE, TA-DAAAAH!

DAN (*beat*): That's the movie?

NEIL: The grabber, buddy boy, the hookeroo. The rest is how the embryo terrorizes the town, lurking at bedroom windows on the lookout for couples making love *without contraception* and rips them to shreds with superhuman strength: *The Revenge of the Unborn*.

DAN: You can't be serious.

NEIL: Why not? Dynamite premise. Topical. Get the Pro-Choicers and Right-to-Lifers screaming bloody murder— zip, free publicity. Do some good visual effects; the embryo'll glow sort of milky white in the dark.

DAN: Neil, it's grotesque, it's the sickest thing I ever heard.

NEIL (*beaming*): Ain't it dogshit! The kids'll eat it up, make an easy fifty million, and here's the beauty part: I own the script, so we're in for a cut of the gross. We'll be rolling in the green stuff, enough to make our very own film at last, and with complete artistic control. Our dream, Danny boy.

DAN: You are out of your mind, Toomie. You come bouncing in here after five years of total fucking silence and try to hustle me with some ludicrous story about Jesus

Christ—I've never heard such an incredibly twisted idea in my entire life—and you behave like we just had lunch together yesterday. I mean, what the hell is the matter with you!

NEIL: Aha, the sleeping beast is roused at last, and he is beautiful to behold. One weekend, Danzer. It won't shatter the whatever . . . delicate equilibrium of your precious existence underground.

DAN (*beat*): Call when you're back from Rhode Island, we'll talk over dinner. Julia's become quite a cook since . . . the time she wasn't such a good cook.

NEIL: I'd rather you didn't tell her I was here.

DAN: Why?

NEIL: You know, wait till the film's all set up, return in a blaze of glory. This is more of a you-and-me thing, okay?

DAN: I don't get it.

NEIL: Then walk in mystery, pal-o'-mine, 'cause there's a whole shitload of stuff I still don't understand about certain things *you* did once upon a time, if you know what I mean, so let's let sleeping dogs lie. (*Pulls out an airline ticket*.) LaGuardia, 5:30 Friday, Eastern, Flight 219 to Bangor, Maine. If you're there, great; if not, no hard feelings, but may generations of your offspring enter the world crippled and mute. (*Starts to exit*.)

DAN: Neil, hang on. You're going to Rhode Island?

NEIL: Yeah.

DAN: To see your folks?

NEIL: My folks?

DAN: That's what you said. To visit your folks.

NEIL (*beat*): I was speaking meta . . . thing, meta . . . you know, what's the fucking word? *Phor*, that's it, meta-*phor*ically. Lay flowers on the grave, a pilgrimage, peckerface, mid-voyage on Spaceship Earth; time to re-collect and pay tribute to things begun—

DAN: Neil?

NEIL (*covering up intense emotion*): Sorry. Been happening lately. I get all . . . things just look so, I don't know, *luminous*. Like a gift. I'm gonna end up a very senti-mental old man, I just know it.

NEIL *exits.* DAN *stares after him, puzzled.*

*   *   *

JULIA *is naturally elegant, even in jeans and work-shirt. She talks to us.*

JULIA: Older? Oh yes, older definitely, with a vengeance. You know, a little jiggle where the flesh used to be tight. My hands: the skin here (*shows the back of her hand*) stays white a little too long when you press it with your finger. Sometimes it feels like the only *real* thing happening to me, getting older. But it has its good points. Like how you finally start to know what you really want out of life (*a*) and that (*b*) you probably won't get it. I mean this in the good sense, recognizing limits, et cetera. You see, I'm one of those people who used to think, "My time on earth matters, I'll live among people who leave the world better than we found it." That was my dream. I hate waking up. I'm not what you call a "morning person," but sooner or later you have to face the day, right? Right. So, what I finally know I want, really and truly want . . . okay, here goes: to be sur-rounded by exquisite and beautiful things all day long.

Oriental rugs, genuine. Handmade terra cotta tiles. Antique furniture. A private white sand beach on the ocean. Vineyards would be nice. Oh, and a limousine with cool leather seats that always smell new. I don't tell Danny, of course. He'd just laugh and tell me I'm trying to fill some middle class spiritual void with pointless possessions. That's how he talks. Oh, I'm sorry, Danny is my husband. Well, it's a little complicated at the moment. He's a film director. Used to be; also complicated. Show me a life and I'll show you a mess, right? I didn't say my name, did I. Typical, Danny first, then me. I'm Julia. Julia Rittman. (*Pause.*) What was I about to say? There was something.

*   *   *

DAN *and* JULIA's *living room—Upper West Side, New York. Comfortable, slightly bohemian, done on a small budget but with warmth and taste. New clothes in boxes and shopping bags on sofa.* TOM *stands in the front door, watching* JULIA. *He wears sunglasses and is extremely good-looking, like a soap opera star, perhaps.*

TOM: I got held up in traffic, it's insane out there. Is he here yet, what's his name?

JULIA: Don't say a word unless you like it. Not exactly what I asked for, but Antonio said leave it to him and so I did and it's awful, right?

TOM: I think it's very, very sexy.

JULIA: Wrong, wrong, wrong, it's supposed to be efficient and professional.

TOM: That's what I mean, it's very efficient and professional.

JULIA: Tom, you are no use at all. Why did I just sit there and let him do this? Now I'll have to go back for the final interview with this whole new thing on my head and it'll look like I'm trying too hard. What about the jacket?

TOM: Take it easy, Julia. It's just a job. If you get it, great, if you don't—

JULIA: I'll kill myself. Head international buyer for the entire jewelry department is not just a job, Tom, it's my destiny: spending millions and millions of dollars buying the best of the best for the best—oh shut up, Julia. You're right. It's just a job. How could they even take me seriously; part-time floor sales is all I've ever done before. It was a joke, the whole application—let me show you the other jacket.

TOM: You really honest-to-God don't see it, do you, what an incredible woman you are: smart, energetic, fun to be with. They gotta be dying to hire you.

JULIA: You're such a sweetheart. Thank you for coming over.

> JULIA *hugs him affectionately.* TOM *responds with a kiss.* JULIA *starts to yield, then turns her head away.*

I think maybe not.

TOM (*regrouping*): So where's the genius?

JULIA: In Maine.

TOM: What's in Maine?

JULIA: Business. Something.

TOM: He's away for the weekend and didn't tell you what he's doing?

14

JULIA: Room to breath. Private space. It's the new regime.

TOM: Bullshit.

JULIA: Change of subject, shaky ground.

TOM (*pause*): When they shoot a criminal in China, they send his family a bill for the bullet. That way he's punished for his crime, and his family's disgraced for bringing an evil person into the world. I read that last week. Been dying to share it with someone. Is this a safe topic?

JULIA: Much better. See how civilized we can be?

TOM (*unplanned*): I love you, Julia.

JULIA (*beat*): Well, I love you too; now drink your wine before it turns to vinegar.

TOM: I know, I know, I promised not to bring it up again, but . . . you and Dan are back together, and that's really great. And you and me are still whatever we are which I'm not sure what that is any more except it's better than nothing, I guess, but . . . I'm sorry.

JULIA: What happens if the criminal's family refuses to pay the bill?

Pause. Tom smiles. The doorbell.

That must be him. Open the red and pour me a glass. *Half* a glass.

JULIA *opens the door to* ADEN, *a precise, diffident man. From behind him bursts* RALPH, *a hulking Yorkshireman who retains strong traces of his North Country accent.*

Ralph, what on earth are *you* doing here?

RALPH: I'm drunk. I'm quite drunk. But I'm not quite drunk enough. Is there any booze about?

JULIA: Sideboard, top right-hand door.

RALPH: In other words, get it yourself, Ralph. Good idea, good idea. (*Sees* TOM.) Do I know you from somewhere?

TOM: I don't think so.

RALPH: Odd, you look bloody familiar. You're not gay by any chance?

TOM: Sorry.

RALPH: No, no, no, don't apologize, neither am I, all that often, but the more possibilities in life, tra-la. *Booze!* Lovely word, that. (*Exits.*)

ADEN: I'm so incredibly sorry about Ralph. He had, well, something of a setback today, and my wife felt he shouldn't be left on his own upstairs. Perhaps I should have called first, but, well, frankly, I wasn't sure I'd ever again have the very good luck to arrange a meeting with—

JULIA: This is Aden Paltz. Aden, Tom Cooper.

ADEN: My God, I didn't introduce myself! It's just that I've never actually met a celebrity before and so I'm . . . did Julia explain?

TOM: You want to meet me, she didn't say why.

ADEN: No, she couldn't have told you that, really, because . . . well, because I didn't tell *her*, my God, your hair!

JULIA: What do you think?

ADEN: What do I think? Gosh. Well, I think it's just nothing like it used to be.

JULIA: Do you like how it looks?

ADEN: Well. It's a little bit as if you'd been sitting across the table from someone you know very, very well, and then you turn to them suddenly and they're Chinese. Actually, I do rather like it.

TOM (*politely*): I have a rehearsal at two.

JULIA (*to* ADEN): Go on, it's all right.

ADEN: Ah. Yes. well now, the thing is, I imagine people ask you for favors just all the time. I mean, they even ask me, and I'm just a philosophy teacher, whereas you, on the other hand, are a *television celebrity*. Julia says you actually have a fan club!

TOM: Teenagers mostly. And bored housewives.

ADEN: Incredible! That's simply . . . well, now, I imagine these fans of yours don't spend a great deal of time thinking . . . about, say, certain things. Except, of course, they must think a great deal of the time about, well, *you*! So, if they were somehow to learn that you were very, very concerned about a particular subject . . . *whales*, for instance, then maybe they'd think they should be concerned about whales too. Julia says they actually write to ask where you buy your clothes.

TOM: Sometimes.

ADEN: Incredible! That's just never happened to me.

TOM (*beat*): What did you, actually, want?

ADEN: I don't know how you feel about nuclear weapons. You might think they're just the most incredibly wonderful things in the entire world!

TOM: What about 'em?

ADEN (*here goes*): Next week, in Central Park, we're having a demonstration. I can't tell you how great it would be if you gave a speech. It needn't be a *long* speech. Only a few words to show your support for nuclear disarmament.

TOM (*beat*): I see.

ADEN: This isn't somehow upsetting you, is it?

TOM: I'm afraid I can't help.

JULIA: Why not?

TOM: Are you in on this?

JULIA: Think what an effect you could have. If I were in your position—

TOM: Our sponsors are ultraconservative. They get very upset when their actors become involved in political issues.

ADEN: My god, I never thought of it as a political issue. Does it really matter if we're blown to pieces by a Russian bomb or an American bomb? If we're dead, we're dead. It seems more of a health issue.

TOM: Sorry, nothing personal, it's just my contract.

ADEN: How incredibly depressing. I always imagined that to be so famous was a kind of wonderful *freedom*. Instead, I'm learning that it's more like a terrible *prison*. I mean, you don't do what *you* want to do; you have to do what *they* want you to do.

RALPH (*reenters with whiskey*): Are we done with the boring bit?

ADEN: I'm taking you upstairs, Ralph. My wife will make supper; you can stay with us tonight.

18

RALPH: Ah, so he said no, eh? Smarter than he looks. Oh face it, Aden, we're a race of children, all of us, great big grown-up children with great big grown-up toys. Forget nuclear weapons. Mere firecrackers to what we'll dream up one day: the Ultimate Toy! Mighty enough to shatter the earth in one fiery bang—only this one can't be tested, you see, because if it works, *finito la commedia*. So there it will sit, gleaming and deadly beautiful in its dark chamber, all us curious children pressed in the doorway staring at the red button aglow on its side, hypnotic, inviting. "Push me, push me," it says. What child could resist? So for Christ's sake, let's at least have a good carry-on while the clock ticks down, eat, fuck, make merry—

JULIA (*furious*): Shut up, Ralph, just shut up; it's not funny and we all know you don't mean it, so what's the point!

RALPH: That's what I love about you Yanks, such passion! At least if you lot push the button first, it'll be done with real feeling.

JULIA: Oh go to hell. If that's what you really think, why not just go back to England and put a bullet through your head.

RALPH: To kill oneself in England would be redundant, my dear.

ADEN: That's enough. (*Explaining.*) His poems were rejected by another publisher today.

RALPH: Yes, yes, I suppose it all comes down to that. Bloody depressing, really. (*Recalls.*) Ah, for you, my dear. (*Takes an envelope from his jacket pocket.*) No sign of allergy. I suspect generalized asthma, but to be safe I'll run a final series of tests next week, when I'm whole of mind and somewhat sober. Bugger 'ell, Doctor Ralph's not going to be sick, is he? Yes, he is. Excuse me. (*Exits.*)

ADEN: I just don't know what to say. I'm so very embarrassed. Julia, Mr. Cooper, you've been incredibly patient.

TOM (*fascinated*): Is that guy, did he say he was a doctor?

ADEN: A very brilliant one. But professionally unwelcome. You see, he doesn't believe that doctors should take money except when offered.

> RALPH *reappears in the hallway arch quietly, unnoticed.*

TOM: Why not?

RALPH (*comes forward*): False alarm, thank Christ. And it's very simple, you see. When a man brings me his suffering, it seems in very poor taste, not to mention positively ghoulish, to say, "Money, my friend, money first, then I'll ease your pain." Oh fuck, here it comes again. If you plan to talk about me, please be good enough to wait until I return. (*Reexits.*)

ADEN: I'd better see if he's . . . dear me. (*Exits.*)

JULIA: Well, it *seemed* like a good idea. You all right? Dinner tonight, my treat?

TOM (*muses*): They come up on the street: "Brad Starkey, is that really you! Can I have your autograph? Is it true Roberta's leaving you for good this time?" I want to shake 'em by the collar and yell, "No, lady, I'm Tom Cooper, the actor, and Roberta's not my wife. It's fiction, lady, make-believe. Can't you see the difference?" But no, I play along, sign my name Brad Starkey. I'm not squawking, hell, I'm onto a good thing, but still, when you think about it, what a weird way to spend your life.

JULIA: The purple jacket. It's more me.

Doorbell. JULIA, *puzzled, rises.*

TOM (*oblivious*): Five days a week. For six years.

JULIA *opens the door.* MICHELLE-MARIE *wedges inside.*

MICHELLE-MARIE: Julia? Julia Rittman?

JULIA: Can I help you?

MICHELLE-MARIE: I'm Michelle-Marie. May I please see Neil.

JULIA: Neil?

MICHELLE-MARIE: I'm not supposed to know he's here, is that the deal?

JULIA: I'm sorry, but I don't think I know you.

MICHELLE-MARIE: He didn't even mention me? Great! I'm his wife. You know, Michelle-Marie Toomie.

JULIA: Oh my God, Neil! You're Neil's wife!

MICHELLE-MARIE: Hey, you don't have to do a whole number here. American Express verified a charge from New York last Wednesday, so I figured it out all by my little ol' self.

JULIA: This is all starting to fit together. I have a feeling, in fact I'm quite sure, Neil is with my husband in Maine.

MICHELLE-MARIE: May I have the number, please.

JULIA: Danny didn't leave one. He said he'd call when he had a chance.

MICHELLE-MARIE: What'd Neil tell you—I was stupid or something? Never mind. Just tell him I'm at the HoJo Motel over on whatever it is, and I'd really appreciate it if he'd be in touch with me like real soon. It's pretty heavy duty, okay?

JULIA: I don't have the number. Why wouldn't I tell you if I did?

MICHELLE-MARIE (*pause*): I'm just trying to figure out, you know, the next step kind of thing. Sorry, these pills. I'm a little whaddyacallit . . . (*spots* TOM.) Hi.

JULIA: Sorry . . . Tom Cooper.

TOM: How do you do.

MICHELLE-MARIE: Shitty, thanks. (*Revelation*.) Brad Starkey! Oh man, I must be hallucinating. It in't the pills, is it? You *are* Brad Starkey!

TOM: In the flesh.

MICHELLE-MARIE: Wow, first day in New York! I haven't missed a show in five years hardly. But I cannot believe that whole business with Roberta walking out. So what if you drink a little; jiminy, your kid died, that's a personal tragedy. My pa drank all his life *and* he beat up on Mama, but she didn't just up and slam the door in his face.

RALPH (*reenters towards* MICHELLE-MARIE): For me? Bit young, but it's the thought that counts. What's your name, love?

ADEN (*directly behind*): Ralph, that's enough.

RALPH (*deflated*): Forgive me, dear Julia. We really ought to make love one day. I'm awfully good, you know.

22

MICHELLE-MARIE (*taking camera from bag*): Would you mind if someone took a picture of us together, Mr. Starkey? No one'll ever believe me without I show 'em evidence.

TOM: Maybe I'll come with you guys, if that's okay. (*To* JULIA:) I'll call after rehearsal. Dinner. Movie.

Exit ADEN, RALPH *and* TOM.

MICHELLE-MARIE: Oh man, that was so great, I went right out of myself for a whole entire minute. How do you know Brad Starkey?

JULIA: Michelle . . . may I ask . . . has something happened with Neil? What are you doing here?

MICHELLE-MARIE: You're just exactly as beautiful as he said. I thought he was trying to get me all hot and bothered is all. You know him and his stories: on and on and on about the wild old days, "Before Michelle," he calls it. I call it B.M.; you should see his face, boy, that really gets him.

JULIA: You've been crying, haven't you. Your eyes—

MICHELLE-MARIE: I could sure do with a cup of coffee. These pills, see . . .

JULIA: I'll be right back. (*Starts out.*)

MICHELLE-MARIE: Don't leave me alone.

JULIA: Michelle, what is going on?

MICHELLE-MARIE: He wouldn't listen. Kept putting it off and putting it off. I told him, I said, "Neil, baby, just let 'em test you, it in't right, all these dizzy spells." But you know him, stubborn as a mule. (*Holds out a large negative.*)

23

JULIA (*takes it*): What's this?

MICHELLE-MARIE: The CAT scan. The lighter part's his skull, and all in there where it's dark, that's the tumor part. It's just about everywhere. That's why they can't operate. Malignant.

JULIA: Neil? Oh Jesus.

MICHELLE-MARIE: I really think he ought to be told about this, don't you? Please, just give me the number.

*   *   *

> MICHELLE-MARIE *talks to us, smoking a joint*.

MICHELLE-MARIE: When you do a lot of driving like I do . . . see, where we live everything is pretty far away from everything else (*tokes*) . . . like your house is here . . . and the mall is over there . . . school is over here—Timmy starts first grade next year; he's my first-born, real, real smart (*tokes*) . . . oh, and tennis is like way across the valley, so when you ride the freeways a lot of hours every day you start to realize how much of your life you spend being not really *at* somewhere but between somewhere and somewhere else. These pills, phew (*tokes*) . . . one every four hours, the guy said—one did nothing for this girl, it's three at a time or forget it, see; even at the very best of times I'm not what you'd call heavily into reality. Father Bonelli says it's not a good thing to run away from life and okay, maybe he's got a valid point, but on the other hand, what the heck does a priest know about life (*tokes*) . . . oh, and this woman, she lives next door and wears these like peasant blouses, Heidi in Sun City, it is too entirely bizarre . . . we have a great house . . . I think she makes pottery, yeah, that would explain the blouse, but her husband, what an unbelievable asshole—always grabbing my tush and going "Honk-honk, quality control, you pass." You know the type . . . but he's our neighbor so what are you gonna do. Calls my husband "Ace", "Hey, Ace, I sure love to grab your wife's ass." I mean you don't go 'round doing things like that when you're a grown-up . . . I am a mother of three, I am a grown-up for pity's sake (*tokes*) . . . the thing about reality, like how I was saying . . . sometimes it can be very, very painful, and who needs more pain; so it's Pilltown for me, and Smokeville, and Powder City—"The Big Rock Candy Mountain." My mama used to sing that. (*Beat*.) Mama. (*Beat*.) Without a little help your heart could burst with the pain (*tokes*) . . . and then like I'll just pull up to the place where I was driving to and presto, like magic, suddenly there I am: somewhere! You know what I'm saying?

*　　*　　*

Housefront and patio, Maine—weathered, elegant facade of a gracious home. There is a small patch of sky visible to one side. GINA, *topless, spreads lotion on her body.* DAN, *across the patio, tries to read a script. A moment passes. Enter* AVRAM, *a vigorous, commanding Israeli who is used to being the center of his world. He is immediately followed by* SYLVESTRE, *an ancient, frail butler carrying a silver tray with a dome cover.*

AVRAM: Sunshine in Maine and breakfast by the ocean, how fun! Put it there, Sylvestre, we can serve ourselves this morning. (*Kissing* GINA's *head*.) Thank you, Sylvestre, you may go now. (*Beat*.) What!

SYLVESTRE: Oui, monsieur. (*Exits*.)

AVRAM: It is simply remarkable the energy I find since I stop smoking the cigarettes. I need only four hours sleep in the night, and I make love for two hours without a rest, yes, Gina?

GINA: You're in great shape, hon.

AVRAM: And who played a very fine game of chess last night? You know, Daniel, in the end game you had me for a moment eating my fingers I was so nervous.

GINA: *Nails*, Av, finger*nails*, and it's biting, not eating.

AVRAM: Ach, this English, so many idioms. After six languages is such a confusion.

DAN: You played a pretty decent game yourself, Avram.

GINA: He let you win?

AVRAM (*smiles*): Daniel *earned* his victory. Even when the situation looked hopeless he fought so hard. Always in this moment you learn the most about a man's character.

GINA: Avram's ranked ninety-fourth in the world, aren't you, pooch.

DAN: Don't I feel silly. I thought I'd won fair and square.

AVRAM: Ginelah, I don't like this without the top. Put it on please. (GINA *obeys simply*.) So, I think we must begin the breakfast without your very original friend (*lifting dome*). What is this thing? (*Furious*.) Impossible! I do not put up with such a nonsense. (*To intercom:*) Sylvestre, are you there? Answer me!

SYLVESTRE (*his voice*): J'attend, monsieur.

AVRAM (*yells into intercom*): What did you make in this food? The eggs are scrambled hard like a stone and the toast is from this stupid white kinds of bread—are you trying to destroy on purpose my entire weekend with new friends?

SYLVESTRE (*his voice*): Juliette, she make the breakfast today, monsieur.

AVRAM (*into the intercom*): This excuse is not interesting. Wait in the kitchen. (*To the others:*) I will see to this myself. The man is an idiot. Next time I shoot him.

AVRAM *starts off with the tray.*

GINA: *Fire* him, hon, and take it easy, it's only breakfast.

AVRAM: Yes, and next is the lunch, and then the dinner, and before you can turn your back around, everything is completely going into the bathroom.

AVRAM *exits.* GINA *yells after him.*

GINA: *Down the toilet!* (*To* DAN:) In case you hadn't noticed, food is a major event in Avram's life.

DAN (*pleasant*): We are what we eat.

GINA: Give me a break.

GINA *applies more lotion.* DAN *looks towards her, away from her, towards her.*

DAN: Want a hand with that? Your back?

GINA: Sure. (*Indicating the rules.*) My *back*. And do it even, okay—I hate blobs. (DAN *applies lotion.*) So what's it like having a nervous breakdown?

DAN (*beat*): Pardon me?

GINA: Sounds so great. Unplug all the circuits and just veg out.

27

DAN: Who told you about that?

GINA: Whoops. No one's supposed to know, is that the deal? It was Avram.

DAN: I'm just surprised he knows anything at all about me. Two days we've been here and he hasn't said a word about film.

GINA: Don't let him fool you with that charming asshole routine. He notices everything, remembers everything, and he always, repeat, *always* gets what he wants. He's even killed people. It's true. Not like *murder*, just 'cause Israel, they all do it over there, no big deal: waste an Arab and go to lunch.

DAN: What other skeletons of mine did Avram dig out of the closet?

GINA: Let's see. Eleven films in school. Moved to L.A. with your friend. Some TV work. What else—oh yeah, tried to sell a movie script, you to direct, no luck. Then loony bin, back to New York and nothing since.

DAN: As in five years of teaching equals nothing. Interesting.

GINA: Do my shoulders. Mmmm, that feels great. You've got good hands.

DAN: Thank you.

GINA: Where'd you find those people, they couldn't've been actors.

DAN: What people—you saw my films?

GINA: Well, three of them. Avram had a screening last week, just him and me.

DAN: And the verdict?

GINA: Kind of weird, I thought. Just people talking at the camera, doing crazy things. At least they were short. Hey, that's not a putdown, only I couldn't figure out why you were so interested in all those losers.

DAN: I was told that's what America was crying out for: short, weird films about losers.

GINA: By the way, I'm not into sarcasm.

DAN (*beat*): Everyone's a miracle, Gina. A world complete with a story to tell. If you don't listen, if you don't pay attention—

GINA: Right, like there's a zillion trillion people in the world and I'm supposed to give 'em all equal time? No wonder you landed in the nuthouse.

DAN (*beat*): Yes. (*Smiles.*) No wonder. (*Returns the lotion.*) All done.

GINA: Well, Danny, I wasn't sure at first, but I think I really like you, so here's the deal. Avram's just waiting to see when *you'll* bring up the film—cat and mouse, he loves it. But I'll tell you this: he digs you a lot, and once he's on your side he's unbelievably loyal. But he's also very possessive, and I mean like mad crazy jealous, so tell your hotshot friend to cool it with the nighttime fun and games or he'll blow the whole deal here.

DAN: Oh man, did Neil pull something?

GINA: That depends on what you call climbing into my bed naked at one in the morning. If you and Avram hadn't been downstairs playing chess, beaucoup heaviness would've come down, and we're talking probable extreme violence, okay.

We hear, then see NEIL, *who enters singing.*

NEIL: "Zip-a-dee-doo-dah,
Zip-a-dee-ay . . ." (*etc.*)
Ever see *Jungle Book?* Classic Disney. How that man understood the animal kingdom.

GINA: That's not from *Jungle Book*. It's *Song of the South*.

DAN: Neil.

NEIL: Dan.

DAN: Cool it, all right? I didn't come up here to waste a weekend, so just cool it altogether, or I call Julia and head home.

NEIL: I got the doors confused. Went out for a leak, thought I was back in my room, they all look the same in the dark; that's the truth, I swear.

Enter AVRAM *with* SYLVESTRE, *who carries the same tray as earlier.*

AVRAM: This time I make sure we have no mistakes. And, after breakfast, with such a nice sunshine, I make a suggestion . . . *what*, Sylvestre?

SYLVESTRE: Voulez-vous quelque chose d'autre?

AVRAM: Non, non, leave us alone now, and next time je vous terminez absolument, comprenez?

SYLVESTRE: Oui, monsieur. (*Exits.*)

AVRAM: Stupid man. Yes, and after food, we go into my boat. Neil says you are an expert sailor, Daniel, and this is so lucky for me because I buy a new spinnaker sail and will need an extra hand on board to help me shake it up.

GINA: *Down*, sugar, shake it *down* means try it out.

30

AVRAM: Isn't she simply fabulous!

DAN: How about if we talk about the film. I heard a rumor that's why we were up here.

NEIL: Hey, Danzer, what's the big rush? Chow into some breakfast, cop some rays, hit the high sils, hyzils, *boat*, go on the boat.

AVRAM: What would you like to know about the film, Daniel?

DAN: Are you for real about putting up the money, or are you one of those guys that just likes to get off hanging around artists?

NEIL: What Danny means—

AVRAM: Be such a good girl and serve us, Ginelah.

> AVRAM *gestures them to the table.* GINA *serves from side stand.*

You would like to know then if I am serious to give you money for this horrible film, yes?

GINA (*serving*): *Horror*, Av. It's a *horror* film.

AVRAM: You know, in the Negev Desert I make thousands of acres to grow with food, but to own so much land, impossible. So I like very much in Maine I can own this estate. Only one thing I like not so much. The taxes. Many thousands every year. What to do, though, always this question. Soon we have here an election for County Commissioner. This man then chooses the Board of Tax Assessors. If the Board is, what to say, *friendly*, my taxes stay where they are. Otherwise, up. So, if I help a man to become County Commissioner, perhaps he helps me in return, you see?

DAN: I'm lost. Weren't we just talking about film?

AVRAM: An acquaintance of mine, Mr. Gunther, is now slightly ahead in the polls, but the election will be so close. A short film of his better qualities . . . thirty seconds long, shall we say? This he can use to expose himself on the television.

DAN: You want us to make a campaign spot for your friend Mr. Gunther in order to keep your taxes down—is that what I'm hearing?

AVRAM (*beams*): Exactly! You see, Ginelah, I never misjudge a man. I pay, of course. But more important, it gives you practice to direct after so many years away. Then we make your . . . horror film, and everyone shares the success!

DAN: Un-fucking-believable. Toomie, did you know this was the setup?

NEIL (*shrugs*): But why not? Get the old moves back.

DAN: I'll tell you my problem here, Av. This Mr. Gunther friend of yours, didn't I read in the local papers that he embezzled three-and-a-half million dollars from a pension fund?

AVRAM (*shrugs*): This I don't know about.

DAN: And isn't he the one who advocates the electric chair for anyone who performs an abortion—which seems, I don't know, a little on the extreme side, don't you think?

AVRAM: In the film, better we don't say these things. More we show the good side. He was I think in the Marines. This is useful. (*Beat.*) Ah, you make a joke to me. Why is such a thing funny?

DAN: It's not, Avram. It's not the least bit funny that you don't give a flying fuck what this Gunther character stands for as long as you get your taxes down. Or that someone, anyone, in this case *me*, might care how their work is used.

AVRAM (*puzzled*): You need from me some help. I ask a small thing in return. This is only business, no?

DAN: Oh yes, very tidy. I need money, so I do a small favor to show I'm a good soldier, and in return I get to make your "horrible" film, and then in some mythical distant future, if you still happen to feel like it, *finally* I get to make the film *I* want to make. Well I'm sorry as hell, Avram, but how much shit do you expect a man to walk through before he's allowed to get home?

AVRAM: This depends I think how much he wants to get home. I have other projects we can discuss—

DAN: Save your breath. I've been here before. Yeah, I spent quite a few wonderful years trying to prove myself to people like you. I *needed* them. I don't anymore. May I call New York?

GINA: There's a phone in the atrium.

DAN *goes. A brief silence.*

AVRAM: Like a man on an island by himself, eh, Ginelah? Fascinating. I think we must make this film without him.

NEIL: No! (*Beat.*) You can't do that. It's my script.

AVRAM: Then you find the money.

NEIL: He's nervous is all. Been away from the action for a while. Trust me, Avram, he's the best there is. When he's cooking, no one touches him. It's crazy he's not working. It's just evil.

AVRAM: Why is this so important to you?

NEIL: A tree in the forest, it falls, and everything's changed. It's important, okay, never mind why. I'll talk to him. (*Flash*.) Talk—?

AVRAM: It is for friendship, then? This is touching.

NEIL (*spellbound*): Corn! That's the smell! Fresh baby corn! The breath, a young girl when you first kiss her. I was trying to tell Danny that smell . . . this is, Jesus, graduate school, first semester . . . we'd just met; three days and nights we walked, all over the city—Williamsburg, Red Hook, up into Harlem . . . two minds, like *that* (*snaps fingers*), talking about everything under the sun: cars, music, politics, getting laid. . . . Fresh baby corn! I couldn't find the way to describe her breath . . . my very first kiss. Anita Larsen. "Poodles," they called her. Lily of the Valley cologne. Tiny perfect little powder blue mohair titties in my hand. Silver crucifix right here (*points to his sternum*). "Poodles"!

AVRAM (*beat*): This is a kind of dog, no?

NEIL (*sudden*): Yeah, me and Danny in the coffee shop, third morning, exhausted, talked out. He said, "Then what happened?" you know, like we were two characters in a story, and I said, without even thinking, "Then they made a movie." Crazy. Neither of us knew dick about film—he was history, I was moral philosophy— but we took one look at each other and *bango*, that was it; ran outta there like a couple of lunatics, rented a cheapo camera, took off in my rusted-out VW, and headed west until we ran across Amelia Morgenwasser, living in a trailer park in Pennsylvania—

GINA: *Amelia!* We saw that one, remember, Av?

AVRAM: This very fat lady, yes.

NEIL: "Three hundred pounds of pink frenzy," that was her business card.

GINA: And all the kites—unreal!

NEIL: Yeah, she adored kites. That string tied to her waist and trailing down: all her idea. Arms out, pink sequined G-string, huge moon-shaped lady teetering at the edge of the trailer roof pretending she was a kite—

GINA: On the *roof,* that's how you did it! I swear it looked like she was up in the sky.

NEIL: She wanted to fly, we *made* her fly! God bless Amelia Mogendas . . . Monegas . . . Monga . . . (*baffled*) what the hell was her name.

DAN (*reenters*): Neil—

NEIL: What was her name, Danny, that first film with Amelia Morgenwasser—that's *it*, Morgenwasser!

DAN: I just talked to Julia. Pack your stuff, Neil. We have to go now.

NEIL (*beat*): What's the matter? Something happen?

DAN: Just pack, Neil. It's time to go home.

*   *   *

NEIL *steps forward and talks to us.*

NEIL: You know the most incredible thing about Jesus? Christ, I mean: that one. Forget the miracles, they don't prove a thing, except maybe he was divine, and who gives a damn about *that* anymore. After all, if he

35

was *Spirit*, what's the big deal with all his suffering here on earth, right, 'cause he knows he's got himself a first-class ticket back to Cloud Cuckooland when the job's done. But, if he was *wholly mortal*, and all he knew he had for certain was this little bit of time here below, then everything he did had to be its own reward. And *still* he chose to live his life as an example . . . a teaching! Think what he proved by that. Well, two things, really. One: that it's a damn hard thing to do. I mean, half the time they'll just nail your ass to a cross for your efforts . . . especially if you're careless about the crowd you run with. But the second thing, and this is the truly amazing part: he proved *it can be done*—to live your life according to some transcendent and eternal values, and with no hope of reward beyond the literal *doing*. (*Smiles.*) I wonder what my friends would say if they knew I spent so much time thinking about stuff like this. I never tell anyone. You never talk about what really matters.

*   *   *

DAN *and* JULIA'*s living room—present are* DAN, JULIA, NEIL, MICHELLE-MARIE, *and* RALPH, *who holds the CAT scan, then passes it to the others.*

RALPH: According to Dr. Forrestal, it's a rather unusual specimen.

NEIL: How long have I got?

MICHELLE-MARIE: Neil, don't say that.

RALPH: Days. Weeks. Months, perhaps. It's what they call "deep and inaccessible."

JULIA: Meaning what?

36

RALPH: Inoperable. It's the darkish flame-shaped area.

NEIL: This is weird. I don't feel a thing. No pain, no pressure.

JULIA: There has to be something we can do. You read all the time about these new techniques.

RALPH: There's the usual: chemotherapy, radiation, interferon perhaps. It might slow the growth for a time.

JULIA: What about that doctor in Venezuela; we just saw a program about him—

RALPH: Julia, there won't be any miracles. I'm sorry, but you wanted an honest opinion.

NEIL: What am I in for? Is it painful? Tubes and shit? Will they drug me up till I don't even know my own name?

RALPH: I'm not very good at all this. They tell you, "Stress the time left, we're all of us dying," et cetera. Rubbish. We can pretend it'll never come for us, but you can't any more. It's holding your hand. And soon it'll give a little squeeze. Then another. Sorry. Look, if you plan to spend time in the city, I can arrange for you to see Dr. Forrestal. He's remarkably unmercenary for a specialist. Lovely wife.

MICHELLE-MARIE: We won't be needing that, thanks anyway.

RALPH: Right, then, I'm off. Upstairs awaits a nubile young creature, she's all limbs and giggles. Hopefully of age. If you need me . . . (*Starts out.*)

NEIL: What would you do right now in my place?

RALPH (*beat*): Carry on as before. In other words, have a bloody good time. With a Young Republican, oh yes, oh yes—all that radiant optimism, that sweet innocent confidence, might rub off and add years to one's life. (*Remembers*.) Ah yes, Aden made me promise to apologize for the other day. So, apologies. It were that television chap, you see. Nice people seem to bring out the worst in me. He's agreed to speak at the rally, you know. Aden finds him captivating, can't think why. Must be that it's years since he met anyone with virtually no brains. I can't believe I said that. I'm terribly sorry. Bloody awful business. (*Exits*.)

NEIL (*beat*): Who's up for a movie?

MICHELLE-MARIE: We'll be leaving in the morning.

NEIL: We will? Where was I when this decision was made?

MICHELLE-MARIE: Neil, baby, we can't stay here, this in't our home.

JULIA: We have a spare room. You're welcome to use it for a few days.

MICHELLE-MARIE: It's the children. My sister's going buggy. They're a real handful at this age.

NEIL: I need some time to think things over.

MICHELLE-MARIE: You can think just fine at home, sugar. I'll fix up the den all nice and cozy.

NEIL: I'm going to stay in New York for a while. I need the grime and stink and fucked-up people in the streets. Feels good.

MICHELLE-MARIE: What about Timmy? He's been asking for you every day.

NEIL: I'm not sure I want my children to see me dying.

MICHELLE-MARIE: We'll talk about it later.

NEIL: Don't you ever fucking listen, Michelle? This isn't Channel Six, you just flip the dial and get a better program in a minute. I told you I'm staying here. You do whatever you want.

MICHELLE-MARIE (*rises; a summons*): Neil.

> MICHELLE-MARIE *exits towards kitchen.*
> NEIL *trots after her.*

JULIA: What do we do?

DAN: Do?

JULIA: We can't just sit around here helpless and watch while Neil dies.

DAN: You heard Ralph. You want a second opinion.

JULIA: Kansas, was it? I've been trying to . . . one of the very first films. We got drunk . . . no, first Neil met that cattle auctioneer at the burned-out Texaco station. (*Smiles.*) He could always do that, couldn't he, start talking to a total stranger and ten minutes later they were best friends. You were too shy. You'd sort of lurk at the side and watch like a cat to see if he'd found a good person for a film. It wasn't Kansas . . .

DAN: Earth to Julia, come in.

JULIA: It *was* in a bar. You said, "The three of us will always work together. Let's swear it. Never to slip from the best that's in us." And we drank a toast. It was perfect. Remember that?

DAN (*beat*): I don't.

JULIA: Danny!

DAN: I'm sorry. We made so many films . . .

They exchange a look. Pause.

JULIA: You could have lied.

DAN: Is that what you want?

JULIA: Why is he dying? Why?

DAN: How 'bout a drink?

JULIA: I went to church today.

DAN: You went *where*?

JULIA: I had to talk to a minister.

DAN: Julia, you've never been to church in your life.

JULIA: Wrong. In my innocent days, pre-Daniel, I had moments of faith. Almost.

DAN: We've never lived as if answerable to a higher power, and to begin now, just because a friend happens to be dying . . . it's dishonest, Julia. And easy, and small. We owe Neil better than that.

JULIA: You're not in class—don't lecture me. I can't help what I feel. If there's a reason he lived, there must be a reason he's dying.

DAN: He has a fucking brain tumor, that's the reason.

JULIA: I won't argue. We made new rules, remember? No putdowns. Crazy thoughts allowed.

DAN: It's great patching up a marriage. Such ease. Such familiarity. (*Pause.*) I'm sorry. Did you find yourself a minister?

JULIA: Yes.

DAN: Good. What'd he have to say?

JULIA (*beat*): God takes us all at our appointed hour.

DAN: Brilliant! And these guys get paid?

JULIA: Let's forget the whole thing.

DAN: Julia, you're too damn smart to take comfort from that kind of sanctimonious twaddle.

JULIA: Who says I did? See that, you never let me finish. I told him he was an arrogant horse's ass.

DAN (*delighted*): You didn't!

JULIA: No, I didn't. But I thought it. There I am, sobbing my guts out and all he can offer—you know what he said? There's a book about dying. Can you believe it! *The Five Responses to Death*, something like that. I wanted to throw him through the stained-glass window.

DAN: What *did* you say?

JULIA: Stop smirking.

DAN: No, really, this is getting interesting.

JULIA: You can make me laugh now, but it won't change what I feel . . . what I *know*. And I *know* this is all happening for a reason.

DAN: All right! But for now Neil is still very much alive, and he won't want to see us drag around here as if we're already in mourning.

JULIA: What do you suggest?

DAN: Get on with it. Routines, little things: how was your weekend, the hair looks nice, any word on the job, any messages?

JULIA (*beat*): Thank you for the hair. You mean it? Good. (*Trying.*) I have a final interview Thursday. No messages. This doesn't exactly feel natural.

DAN (*explodes*): I could kill the son of a bitch! After all this time, crashing back into our lives with a brainful of rot. You know what I'd really like to do right now? Just sneak out of here, go to Mexico, you and me, leave him a note: "We didn't ask for this, asshole, it's your problem—deal with it."

JULIA: I think the minister said something about this. It's called denial. Maybe we should get that book after all.

They embrace on the couch.

DAN: When he's gone, you and me will be the only ones left who remember the glory days. Then one day we'll go. And then . . . what's left?

JULIA: There's the films.

DAN: Ah yes, the films. (*Rueful.*) The films.

NEIL (*reenters*): Few pills, she'll be fine. So, what's playing at the Roxy?

JULIA: This is happening to her too, Neil. You needn't be such a bastard about it.

NEIL (*beat*): Too late to change now. (JULIA *goes.*) What's she so pissed off about? Hell, she ended up with *you*, didn't she.

DAN: Maybe that's what she's so pissed off about. Neil, did you know something was wrong?

NEIL: You kidding? A little dizziness, overwork, too much coffee—like that. You wonder, you always wonder. I had this little wart on the tip of my dick once; I even thought maybe— (*Stops.*) Yeah, I knew something was wrong. Bad wrong.

DAN: Why'd you come here?

NEIL (*beat*): Good to see you too, Dan.

DAN: No, why *now*? Why didn't you come sooner?

NEIL: Is it a game? You have a nervous breakdown and split, I chase after, beg you to come back to L.A., we try to hustle your script for a few more years; then what—maybe another nervous breakdown?

DAN: I started to write a couple times. I didn't mean to just disappear.

NEIL: Nah, you were smart to get out of there before you drowned in shit. I should've done the same.

DAN: You're different. That life never seemed to bother you.

NEIL: You're an incredibly blind fucking fool, Danny.

DAN: You're doing your work, that's what matters.

NEIL: I'm dying, Danny boy, *that's* what I'm doing. Only now the death is literal. This little flame up here, you know what it is? A window on the fires of hell. Oh yes, I jumped in the Great Money River with both eyes open wide, and now it's time to pay and pay.

DAN: Cut the Catholic shit, Toomie. God is dead, remember.

NEIL: Sorry, chief, the Jesuits got here first. There is a God, and He smiled upon us once—long ago, when we honored the Commandments, the unspoken ones, you know. Thou shalt come to thy labor with love in thy heart. Thou shalt never sell thy gift to men of mean and small purposes. Thou shalt make images of the world as you know it to be, both great and small. All that.

DAN: Easy enough when you're too young to know any better.

NEIL: Every day behind the camera these last five years I'd hear "ACTION!" and I'd pray, "Dear Lord which art in Heaven, please make Danny's TV be broken when this shit airs. Let him remember when my heart was in it. Amen."

DAN: Yeah, I'm sure the one to pass judgment on you.

NEIL: Better than a priest. (*Grins.*) That's what's happening here, right? The fallen Catholic wings back to his favorite Wandering Jew for absolution. (*Removes joints and lights one.*) Hey, what do you say we dump the chicks, go out, and get nasty all over town tonight?

DAN: How long are you going to pretend this doesn't hurt?

NEIL: Till the very end, buddy boy. I'm not like your tribe. No Wailing Wall. No suffering Job. Step on the gas, light a joint, and sail off the cliff laughing all the way, ha-ha-ha.

DAN (*grabs the newspaper*): Let's see what's at the movies.

> NEIL *inhales deeply from joint while* DAN *scans the paper.*

NEIL: Fuck cremation, huh? What if the ghost is slow wriggling out. How do we know they don't feel pain—fire might hurt. On the other hand, being all cooped up in a little wooden box underground, me and my claustrophobia.

DAN: What about mummification? A much-neglected option.

NEIL (*laughs*): I got it! Tie a string to my shroud and float me out over the earth like Amelia Morgenwasser. (*Beat.*) That was a great film, Danny.

DAN: Some of them weren't bad, were they.

NEIL (*breaks down*): Oh Christ, Danny, I don't want to leave all this. I'm right in the middle of such beauty and I'm burning all over . . . burning . . .

DAN (*comforts him*): It's okay, man, I'm here.

NEIL: I need poison. Talk to that doctor guy, get me something quick and painless.

DAN: No! I won't help you kill yourself, Neil.

NEIL: Then what *are* you going to do? Hold my hand and tell me it's okay, it's okay? Make a film about it maybe, *Neil Dying*. (*Pause*.) Danny! Fuck my dying. Let's make a film, just hit the road and find someone, like in the old days. There's a million stories out there and I have time left, enough to make one more for the gods, one last act of grace I can carry upstairs to show 'em I never lost it. (*Beat*.) Don't *think*, you ponderous fuck, just say yes. For *me*, Danny, do it *for me*.

ACT
TWO

DAN *and* JULIA's *living room*—TOM *explains with great conviction, while* JULIA *packs things into a scruffy backpack.*

TOM: *Uncertainty!* That's really what the whole book . . . take the Renaissance, for instance, the Enlightenment . . . I forget what else, but suddenly mankind makes this like amazing leap forward, and *why*? Because these great minds come along and fuse all the small, unconnected ideas lying around into one coherent, exciting new way to look at the world . . . which he says is like a huge pile of dry wood being lit up all of a sudden, and he calls these periods—

JULIA: *Years of Fire.*

TOM: You've read it?

JULIA: Only up to there. It was pretty heavy going.

TOM: Tell me about it. An hour to read one page, then I have to go back and underline. I didn't even know he wrote books until that weird doctor guy told me. I

mean, Aden Paltz: one of the major top-line phi-
losophers in the country, but does he ever toot his horn,
no way. He's so, like, I don't know, incredibly, somehow, modest.

JULIA: You're even starting to talk like him.

TOM: I can't believe I'm bothering you with this when—

JULIA: It's nice to see you so enthusiastic.

TOM: You have enough to deal with. Danny going off. Your
friend . . . well.

JULIA: That's my problem, Tom.

TOM: You really don't mind? (*Pause.*) Okay, then there's
these other periods—Aden thinks we're in one right
now—he calls them "years in the desert"—because
there's only these small, unconnected ideas in the world
and no truly great minds to gather them into a pile and
set them alight. So it's like walking through a desert
now, and what we have to do, you and me, you know,
just regular people, is carry a small coal burning in our
minds—he calls it "clear thought"—and we have to
feed that coal with the best ideas we can find, like
gathering twigs in the sand. But the thing is, we may
just die on our way across the desert and our little coal
will go out. That's the uncertainty part; God, he puts it
so beautifully. It's all about how to keep going forward
in spite of the uncertainty, to make ourselves get up
every day and walk a little further because, well, it
could be any one of us who reaches that pile of wood,
the next "great minds," and our little insignificant coal
will touch off the coming "years of fire." Do you see:
each and every one of us is potentially responsible for
the fate of the entire human race. Isn't that the most
incredible idea?

ADEN (*enters with a coffeepot*): It's hot. I don't know if there's enough for three whole cups.

TOM: Should I call Hector? See if there's anyone in the park yet?

ADEN: You're not scheduled to speak until one.

TOM: People may arrive early. I'm really nervous. I haven't played a live audience for six years.

> TOM *exits to the kitchen.* ADEN *stands with coffee.*

JULIA: You've made quite a convert.

ADEN (*pouring*): Tom? Yes. Actually, I'm very concerned about his behavior lately. It's almost, in a way, fanatical.

JULIA: It's just the speech, actors get like that. He'll be fine.

ADEN: He's such an incredibly nice man. In a way, he's probably the nicest man I've ever met. So this may sound just horribly ungrateful, which I don't mean at all, but it's very hard not to notice that Tom has, well, an incredibly tiny mind. I'm not saying it's a *bad* mind. I mean, he thinks about these very, very tiny things, and very often he's entirely right about them, but they are, on the whole, very, very *tiny*. And what I've noticed about minds like his is that when you put a very *large* idea into them, there's simply no room left for certain other thoughts which might be far more important than he realizes.

JULIA: What are you getting at?

TOM: The sponsors of his show threatened to take action if he speaks in public today.

JULIA: One of their major stars?

48

ADEN: He's managed to upset them terribly. In an interview yesterday he referred to them as blind and ignorant morons.

JULIA (*delighted*): Tom! I didn't know he had it in him.

ADEN (*beat*): Tom is not an enormously gifted actor, is he? I mean, if he were to lose his job, he might find it very hard to make a living. And I would feel responsible.

JULIA: You didn't force him to do this, Aden.

ADEN: No, I didn't put a gun to his head and say "Speak today or else." But I did put an *idea* into his head and, well, ideas are these things that actually make us act in certain ways. Which means we're responsible for the ones we pass along. If I didn't believe that, how could I teach?

MICHELLE-MARIE (*entering through the front door*): Are they here?

JULIA: They went to get equipment.

MICHELLE-MARIE: Just tell me right out, did they leave already?

TOM (*reenters*): Hector said to get over there *now*! It's unbelievable, two hours till the rally and already there's ten thousand people.

> MICHELLE-MARIE *has meanwhile exited to search other rooms.*

ADEN: Incredible. I'll just get my wife and we'll all walk to the park together.

JULIA: I'm not coming.

ADEN: Oh. I see. Well.

49

JULIA: Maybe later.

MICHELLE-MARIE *reenters, agitated.*

TOM (*bustling*): It'll be on the news tonight in case. (*To* ADEN:) We'll go through the speech one more time on the way over. (*Stops. To* MICHELLE-MARIE:) I'm very sorry about your . . . I signed some pictures . . .

TOM *holds them out from his briefcase.*

MICHELLE-MARIE: Pictures? Oh. Yeah, right, thanks.

TOM *expected more. He and* ADEN *go.*

MICHELLE-MARIE: I don't believe they're doing this. What happens if Neil needs attention when they're miles from a doctor?

JULIA: I know.

MICHELLE-MARIE: You want them to go, don't you?

JULIA: What I want right now doesn't really matter.

MICHELLE-MARIE: Look, I know you think I'm a little, what, like ignorant or uneducated or something, not quite in your league? Well, fine, but I am his wife, and I don't want him running off to the drop-end of no-where. It's suicide, Julia, and suicide is a sin in my religion. (*Takes pills out.*)

JULIA: Want some water for those?

MICHELLE-MARIE: See that—like I couldn't get myself a glass of water if I wanted one. I was a waitress, you know; I served the public.

JULIA: This isn't easy for you, I know that. But it's not easy for me, either.

MICHELLE-MARIE (*beat*): So it's true, then. You still love him.

JULIA: Neil? Are you serious?

MICHELLE-MARIE: It's cool. I'm not the jealous type. We could be friends, you know.

JULIA: What nonsense has Neil been feeding you?

MICHELLE-MARIE: For your information, Julia, Neil is not the first college guy I's ever with, not by long, long shot. I am very familiar with the college situation including the Big Man On Campus, in't that what you call it, B.M.O.C.? So, okay, Danny's suddenly the Big Man Hotshot Film Director and Neil's just li'l ol' Number Two. Hell, I'd 'a probably dumped Neil for someone like him too; it's human nature.

JULIA: I hate to burst your bubble, Michelle, but none of us was ever an "item" in school. We made films together. We were a team.

MICHELLE-MARIE: Neil said you were in love with him.

JULIA: Love! We had one date, all of which we spent talking about Danny.

MICHELLE-MARIE (*beat*): He is so full of shit, isn't he? Why does he always have to go and tell stories like that, it's so darn juvenile.

JULIA (*beat*): Danny back then . . . he was blessed. Like he couldn't get over just being in the world. It was so infectious. Me . . . I was the assistant. The idea he'd ever take me seriously . . . in that way. In any way. Except Neil, he knew all along, 'cause it was him, after school I mean, when the two of them moved to L.A., he was the one who called. Danny was feeling down and Neil thought maybe I could cheer him up if I flew out. I

51

thought he was nuts. But of course I went. And Danny
. . . he just lit up. Amazing. 'Cause of me. And for a
while, it was so good. Was was was. Jesus, listen to
me—sounds like a funeral oration.

MICHELLE-MARIE: Neil loves my breasts.

JULIA: Pardon me?

MICHELLE-MARIE: "Super-titties," he calls 'em. You gotta
admit, they ain't bad for three kids. I nursed 'em all,
you know.

JULIA: They'll thank you one day, I'm sure.

MICHELLE-MARIE: Boy is it nice to have a regular old con-
versation with someone. That's what I miss here.
Friends. Just drop on by for a jaw, a cup of coffee, like
in the commercials. What's the one—"Here's to good
friends, tonight . . ."—no, wait, that's beer; what's the
coffee one? I love the commercials. They put an awful
lot of thought into some of them.

JULIA (*coffee cup*): Help yourself. Only moments ago that
cup was held between the lips of Brad Starkey himself.

MICHELLE-MARIE: I love the kind of humor you have.
(*Moves to* JULIA.) The three of you are really close,
aren't you. That must be nice.

JULIA: Feeling better?

MICHELLE-MARIE: I want him home with me, Julia. Isn't
that normal? I'm awake all night thinking and thinking
what's the right thing to do. I wish there was a switch to
turn your damn brain off.

JULIA: In the end, I think it has to be up to Neil how he
chooses to live the time he has left.

MICHELLE-MARIE: It's up to God, Julia, that's the only one it's up to, and I'm not about to let Neil commit the worst sin of his life and get sent straight to hell for it. Please help me. Just swear how he asked Dan for poison. It's the truth, so you won't be giving false testimony. The lawyer told me contemplated suicide is grounds to have him declared mentally incompetent, and then he'd have to come home in my custody. You just keep 'em busy when they get back and I'll call the police—

JULIA: Isn't that going a little far?

MICHELLE-MARIE: What all else can I do? He's the only good thing ever happened in my life. Just tell me how to get him back.

JULIA: You poor kid.

> MICHELLE-MARIE *leans helpless against* JULIA.

MICHELLE-MARIE: He can't stand to be near me anymore. I try to be nice as pie but it only makes him angrier. If I'm not what he wanted, why didn't he just go away after the first night like the rest of 'em? What kind of perfume is that you're wearing?

JULIA (*beat*): Givenchy.

MICHELLE-MARIE: It's nice. You have such beautiful hands. May I do one little thing, Julia. (*Kisses her hand.*) Do you mind?

JULIA (*rising*): I'll put on some fresh coffee.

> MICHELLE-MARIE *holds her tight and kisses her on the lips.*

Stop it, Michelle, what's the matter with you?

MICHELLE-MARIE: I can be wild too, see? You three aren't the only ones. Doesn't that qualify me for membership in this little deal y'all got going here?

JULIA: You're crazy!

MICHELLE-MARIE: And you're full of shit, all of you. The way Neil carried on, I thought I'd be meeting Jesus on the Throne of Glory. What's Danny got that Neil hasn't got—look at this place, you don't even own a dishwasher.

JULIA (*furious*): Neil is nothing without my husband. He's a server and that's all he'll ever be because he doesn't know how to rise above the people around him. I'm sorry, Michelle, but you asked for this!

MICHELLE-MARIE: God help me if I ever have to die among people like you.

Enter DAN *and* NEIL *with camera equipment (16mm) in battered cases.*

DAN: Home from the hunt, and blessings on the film department.

NEIL: This shit has dinosaur tracks on it. I swear to God it's the same camera we used fifteen years ago.

MICHELLE-MARIE (*sweetly*): Hello, sugar. Would you like me to make you some lunch before you leave? Can't let two great big boys drive off without a good hearty meal under their belts.

NEIL (*alert*): What do you say, Dan? She does a wicked bologna on white.

MICHELLE-MARIE: You both set yourselves down and be cozy. I'll have it ready in a jiffy. (*Exits to kitchen.*)

NEIL (*watching*): Red alert! When she gets like that, death and destruction aren't far behind.

JULIA: You were gone a long time. I was starting to worry.

NEIL (*avoiding*): You gonna ask her? See that, he's chicken, he knows I'm right. We made a little bet.

DAN (*plays along*): The school let us have this stuff free. Schneider just opened the storeroom and said help yourself.

JULIA: Why pay? They owe you that much.

DAN: So it *was* you.

NEIL: Ten bucks, Danzer.

DAN: How the hell'd you do it?

JULIA: His article in *Film Quarterly* . . . you wrote it—how awkward if word got out.

DAN: You threatened my boss? Julia, that's not funny.

NEIL (*to* JULIA): Danny never understood how to play hard-ball. (*To* DAN:) Whatever would he do without Julia— ah, now there's an interesting question.

JULIA (*quickly*): Neil, you promised . . . (*Stops.*)

NEIL: It was rhetorical. As in, "How are you getting on with Michelle?" Like that. You know.

JULIA (*a flash*): Michelle. Oh my God, Michelle—excuse me a minute. (*Exits into kitchen.*)

DAN: What's up, Neil?

NEIL: Forget it.

DAN: What'd you promise?

NEIL: You're the prize dumbshit of the Western world, screwing around with a student when you've got her. I fuck up like that, not you.

DAN: Well, buzz buzz buzz.

NEIL: She has to talk to somebody.

DAN: It was one, isolated, stupid indiscretion. And she got even, in case she forgot to mention that little detail.

NEIL: Except she thinks you were trying to say "I want out."

DAN: It's none of your business.

NEIL: You asked. You know, I walked all round the city when I got here . . . same route we took that time . . . looking for things that'll still be here after I . . . (*Stops.*)

DAN: What do you want, me and Julia to declare our marriage a monument to our friendship in memoriam? Anything else we can do for you?

NEIL: You're a difficult son of a bitch.

DAN: Me and Julia, we're trying to work it out.

NEIL: Yeah, fuck it, you're right, none of my bidiless . . . bilid . . . biddi—

DAN: Business.

NEIL: I hear the fucking word inside . . . won't move out. Like when your leg's asleep.

DAN (*feigns casualness*): Man, I'm wasted. What do you say we cop a few zzz's before we split.

NEIL: Don't play nursemaid, fuckhead. I'm fully operational. See that camera? Eight-and-a-half feet. (*Paces off.*) On the nose! I can still focus like a jockey.

MICHELLE-MARIE (*enters quick, stops dead*): Julia's plumb out of luncheon meat, I'll have to pop on down to the superette. Don't y'all go anywhere now.

> MICHELLE-MARIE *rushes out the front door*
> *just as* JULIA *hurries in from the kitchen.*

JULIA: I had to pull the phone cord out of the wall: she's trying to call the police and have Neil arrested for insanity.

NEIL (*beat*): *And* she's a great little housekeeper. I'd better handle this, I've had practice. (*Exits.*)

JULIA: He doesn't look good, Danny.

DAN: He's doing great. Little dizziness, that's natural. Sat him in the lobby for a few minutes, he was fine. This is fucking crazy.

JULIA: Why didn't you think of that before you said yes?

DAN: Come with us.

JULIA: You know I can't.

DAN: We need you. Who's going to be script girl? Who's going to organize? Who do we show off for?

JULIA: Typical. "Hey, I've made up my mind, everyone drop what you're doing and fall in behind."

DAN: It's Neil I'm thinking about. This is our last chance to be together again.

JULIA: Just like the old days, as if nothing's changed.

DAN: Never mind.

JULIA: Neil did not come back here to get any answers from me. (*Beat.*) Look, I'm glad you've found a way to start again, I really am, but there's certain things *I* have to do now too.

DAN: The interview?

JULIA: Yes, dear, I know how seriously you take it.

DAN: That was not a putdown. It's just, in the larger scheme of things it may not be quite as important as . . . you're the one who wanted to do something for him.

JULIA: So this is all for Neil?

DAN: He did ask me.

JULIA: But not me, and he wouldn't, because he knows how it feels to have very little time left. It's not like I'm getting younger.

DAN: You two have been talking up quite a storm, haven't you.

JULIA: Neil and I have a great deal in common.

DAN: How can you not see what you're doing? The same goddamn ritual every year: this little part-time job, that little part-time job, and come spring, like an annual rite of regeneration, you run out and apply for a half-dozen completely impossible jobs. What does it take to wake you up—isn't Neil enough?

JULIA: It's different this time.

DAN: Why?

JULIA: Because certain things I could hope for once, I won't be able to hope for anymore. (*Beat.*) You don't have to understand, just don't stand in judgment. I need this. And if it seems selfish or naive or absurd, well, so be it, because I can't see how it's any more or less reasonable than what you're trying to do, which is make Neil forgive you.

DAN (*pause*): Touché.

JULIA: We're both treading water here. Let's at least try not to push each other under. (*Pause.*) Go, Danny, she's calling the cops.

DAN: I'll phone Thursday, see how the interview went. Good luck.

JULIA: And you. Be brilliant.

DAN: We'll miss you.

JULIA: Good.

DAN: *I'll* miss you.

>   DAN *and* JULIA *embrace.*

>   *   *   *

>   NATHAN *is a rural black man with a sly, gen-*
>   *tle humor. He speaks to us.*

NATHAN: All right then, here's something I know for a actual fact: they is such a place as what you call *hell*. How do I reckon on that? I applied some science to the problem. Yessir, me and my number one man, T.D. Oh, this here's way 'fore your time I'm speaking of, must be forty, fifty years back. I's working the pits, oh yeah, hauling coal up 'round by Carbondale. (*Remembers.*) That's right, I's supposed to say my name out: *Nathan* is my given, title: *Berger*. Yessir, last I heard tell ol' T.D.'s up 'round by Frisco welding on ships. Now he had what you might call sticky fingers, if you know what I'm saying. Things had a way of sticking to 'em. So one day he gets ahold of one of them doodads like what the doctor put around his earhole to listen inside you. And that night me and T.D., we snuckted way down to the bottom of Number Nine Red, old, old mineshaft, must be, oh, five, six hundred foot straight under. Lit us up a candle and put the end of that listening thing up against the rock face to hear what's goin' on below. Holded our breath. Sure enough . . . noises. Real faint, kind of grumbly-type sound, just like what they say about hell. And hell is sure enough what we was hearing. Yessir. Don't understand why no one ever thought to do that particular experiment before, and I don't much care. Now please follow me here. If there's a hell below, can't help but be a heaven above, that's just common sense. So all our trials and tribulations here on earth gonna pass one day, and we all go to our just deserts. See what I'm telling you? *We in good hands,* yessir.

*   *   *

*Field, South Carolina—*NEIL *aims the camera (16mm Eclair) at* NATHAN, *following his movements, while* DAN, *with soundpack and microphone, shoots* NEIL *signals, pulls him gently, nudges him forward according to the frame he wants. The two of them have an ease, an intuitive sense of each other's movements that feels almost like dance. There is a large mound on stage covered with a weathered tarpaulin.*

NEIL: I'm running low, Danny; slate this and I'll reload.

DAN: He has to put more film in the camera, Nathan. We can take it easy for a minute.

NATHAN: I been taking it easy all afternoon.

DAN (*slateboard upside down*): Nathan Berger, tobacco field, South Carolina, reel one, end-slate. (*Click.*)

NEIL (*camera down*): Oh man, wait'll you see this stuff! Mr. Nathan, dyn-o-mite!

DAN: You're doing great, Nathan. We'll get to the dream machine in a minute. The sound is still running, so anything you want to say—go ahead, it's your film.

NATHAN (*nods*): Mister Neil, care for a taste of the good thing? (*Holds bottle.*) Ya'll bought it, might as well relish a drop.

NEIL: Can't drink on the job. After we wrap, you're on.

NATHAN (*to* DAN): That apply to you too, son?

DAN: No, I'll have a little.

NATHAN (*pleased*): There ya go. Grew fond of rum in the Merchant Marine. Mostly the young folks don't know 'bout drinking no more; all 'a that Mary Jane and drugs messing things up. It's the devil's own work, yessir.

DAN: Why's that, Nathan? You think drugs come from the devil?

NATHAN: I know liquor come from God. It's in the Good Book, call it "ambrosia". You don't read nothing about no marijuana in the Bible now, do you. (*Both drink.*) Yessir, everything they is to know on earth it's right there in the Scriptures. All 'a them rocket ships and shooting missiles you hear about . . .even they had mens up on the moon walking 'round funny, but it don't change the underneath things none. Still gotta pee when you're full 'a moisture. Still need loving when the low is on you. Still gotta be keeping busy with this and that.

DAN (*to* NEIL): How we doing?

NEIL: Let's rock 'n roll.

DAN: Ready, Nathan?

NATHAN: Don't see me goin' nowhere.

DAN (*with slateboard*): Sound still running . . .

NEIL: Camera!

DAN: South Carolina, Nathan Berger, reel two. (*Clicks.*) Okay, Nathan, what I'd like you to do is take off the tarp and tell us about your trip, what you were saying back at the bar.

NATHAN: That's a thing I can do for you, certainly. (*Peels tarp.*) Mr. McBride, he let me keep it this side 'a his field free.

> *He reveals a rusted, battered, tireless convertible car up on blocks.*

Now what you see here is my dream machine, which I call it that because I dream about when it's all fix up, I'll sit me down behind the wheel and just gooo!

DAN: Where to, Nathan—you got a route picked out?

NATHAN: All over everywhere. Visit my friends and my childrens.

DAN: You have kids?

NATHAN: Oh my, you ask me that! Why, I have childrens and grandchildrens, and I 'spect some 'a them has childrens too by now.

DAN: How many altogether?

NATHAN: Can't hardly count what I ain't seen. Like it say in the Bible, "Be fruitful and multiply." Well, I begat me a whole orchardful of fruit. Some even dead and gone. Saddest thing on earth, living past your own childrens.

DAN: What if you had a chance to see 'em again—would you do it?

NATHAN: That's crazy talk, son. They's in a place I'll never get to, not after the kind 'a life I lived.

DAN: Maybe you could visit. You know, hop in the car and drive up for a few hours.

NATHAN: Up where?

DAN: Heaven.

NEIL *shoots* DAN *a brief look.*

NATHAN: Heaven! (*Chuckles.*) This ol' heap 'a rust wouldn't make it to Chancellorsville on a towline. Heaven!

DAN: You could make believe. Let's say that car can go any-where you want it to.

NATHAN: You're talking about like in a fairy tale and such?

DAN: Why not? No one's stopping you.

NATHAN: This here gotta be some kind of moving picture. Well now, I 'spect I can do make-believe good as the next man, but I'm starting to wonder 'bout you boys. (*Chuckles.*)

DAN: Tell Neil what you're doing, okay—describe it while it's happening.

NATHAN (*obeys*): Here's me opening the door. Here's me sitting in the driver's seat. Now I'll just close the door like this here. How'm I doin', Mister Neil?

NEIL: You'll be a star across the land, Mr. Nathan.

DAN: Start the car, Nathan.

NATHAN: Well lookee here, I happen to have the real live key right in my pocket. (*Chuckles.*) I'll just put it into the keyhole here. Give it a little turn. (*Smiles.*) My, my, listen to that engine: quiet as a rat pissin' on cotton. Maybe turn on the radio.

DAN: I didn't see any radio in there.

NATHAN: I thought we's doin' make-believe.

DAN: Right, right. What are you listening to?

NATHAN: You don't recognize that, you oughta be ashamed of yourself. Only they's ever one man in the entire world could make the big band sound so fine and his name is called Mr. Ellington. (*Hums a few bars of* "Take the A Train.") Yessir, the Duke hisself, Mr. Basie was a Count, but a Duke is higher than a Count. You didn't think I'd know that, did you. Oh, yes, I'm enjoying myself today.

DAN: Put her in gear and head for heaven.

NATHAN: No problem at all; first gear . . . see that, she start right forward.

DAN (*to* NEIL): Give it motion. (NEIL *highsigns*.)

NATHAN: Second gear, maybe tighten the clutch a tad. Here come third and she's moving along sweet as honey. They laugh when I bought this thing, but look who's laughing now; say, "Nathan Berger!"

DAN: Are you off the ground yet? Tell us what you see.

NATHAN: Road moving away down under me. Lookit over there: Bethune Pond, big enough to get yoursef lost on but it just a itty-bitty puddle from up here, imagine!

DAN: How about birds, must be birds up there.

NATHAN: Yeah, I like that. Here come one, see that, floating on the air right alongside 'a me, big ol' eagle-hawk— you should see his face, eyes bugging right outta his head! What's the matter, eagle, ain't you never seen a flying convertible with a nigger at the wheel! (*Laughs.*)

DAN: Can you see heaven yet?

NATHAN: Don't be rushing me, gotta get past the moon firstly. (*Beat.*) All right, there go the moon. *Now* we look for heaven. Why, I believe I see something right up ahead.

DAN: What is it?

NATHAN: Kind of tollbooth. Don't it figure they'd charge admission. See that, man wave me right on through. Thank you, sir, I 'preciate it. Look, big ol' billboard say "WELCOME TO HEAVEN." Ain't no mistaking where we is now.

DAN: What does it look like up there?

NATHAN: I would have to say it look a lot like South Carolina. Keep the grass trimmed real nice on the verges. Yeah, all in all, it appear to be a very clean community.

DAN (*to* NEIL): We okay on the light?

NEIL: It's fucking miraculous—go!

DAN: You going to visit your children now, Nathan?

NATHAN: Oh, my, it's such a very big place . . . I wouldn't know where to start looking.

DAN: Maybe they knew you were on the way . . . they're in another car looking for you.

NATHAN: Course it is. See, here they come, right up 'side 'a me. They all together, got a convertible car just like mine. Lookit—Lafayette driving. You listen here, Lafayette, keep your eye on the road, else you'll end up doing the same kind 'a nonsense got you up here in the

first place. There's Melanie . . . my, what a pretty little
thing she was. How you been, honey? Course I do, miss
you big as my heart. There's Lonny and Steven . . .
Thomas, smart boy, might 'a gone far he'd 'a had a
whole life . . .

DAN: Are they happy to see you?

NATHAN: Oh, they smiling from here to Sunday morning.

DAN: What do you want to tell 'em, Nathan—now's your
chance.

NATHAN (*moved*): Childrens . . . I love you all. I'll never
understand why you was called home so early. The Lord
must have his reasons, but it broke my heart every
time. Still, I got a whole world inside my head and
you'll be living there forever and ever. Hear me, childrens. I've lived a long life; there were days I thought
they'd never end, and other whole years went by
seemed like in a minute, but no matter. It's how you
live the time you got, that's all what counts. Behold
your daddy and forgive his sins, 'cause he got through it
all whole and happy and with malice in his heart towards no man alive, except maybe one or two I'd 'a like
to bust in the head . . . (NEIL *slumps*.) Mister Neil,
what's happening?

DAN (*sees*): Neil!

NEIL: Take the camera, don't drop it!

DAN (*grabs the camera;* NEIL *is in convulsions*): What is it,
Neil, what's going on?

NATHAN: Look like a epilepta fit. Put somthing in his mouth
he don't swallow his tongue. (*Passes comb.*) They's a
doctor over to Lydia—

DAN (*with the keys*): Take the station wagon; I'll stay with
him.

NATHAN: I don't have a license to drive at this moment.

DAN: I'll be responsible.

NATHAN: Fact is, I ain't drove much 'fore today.

DAN: It's automatic—you can figure it out.

> NATHAN *takes the keys and goes.* DAN *bends over* NEIL, *who is now still, drawing breath in heavy gasps.*

Neil, can you hear me?

> *Thunder.* DAN *pulls a jacket over* NEIL.

NEIL (*dazed*): What was that? The camera—

DAN: It's fine.

NEIL: Can't lose that footage . . . too good.

DAN: Just lie still, don't try to talk.

NEIL: Tired, Jesus. Coffee. The thermos. Can't sleep now, gotta finish.

DAN: No more today. We'll pick it up tomorrow.

NEIL: Tomorrow? Is that a joke? Where's Nathan?

DAN: I sent him for a doctor.

NEIL: Why'd you do that, you dumb shit, we'll lose the light. (*Rises unsteadily.*) We'll shoot some inserts. The field . . . that fence . . .

DAN: No more till you've seen a doctor.

NEIL: We gotta finish.

DAN: We'll finish, I promise. Just rest. I'll get you coffee.

DAN *goes for coffee. Thunder. Both look up.*

NEIL (*looks around, sad*): I'd trade the whole last five years for what we did today. Doesn't it break your heart, all the work we might've done together—

DAN (*at the thermos*): Like a dozen more art films, you mean. More colorful characters God abandoned at the one-yard line? What a great way to end up—pair of underground cinema heroes dragging our aging asses round to special screenings to share our aesthetic vision over bad white wine and chunks of stale cheese.

NEIL: What'd we do that was any better?

DAN: Gave it the old try, the big time. Not our fault no one wanted our script.

NEIL: We'd have gotten that sucker made. We were so damn close.

DAN: You up to helping me pack? It's gonna rain. (*Holds out cup.*) What?

NEIL (*simply*): Why'd you run away?

DAN (*beat*): Take your coffee.

NEIL: Fuck the coffee, you gotta talk to me while I still got something left up here to understand with. Don't turn away, Danny. Why'd you give up?

DAN (*beat*): I didn't give up. I decided to do something else with my life.

NEIL: So why weren't you in touch? What the hell were you hiding from?

DAN: There's no point. If I thought you'd understand I'd have written you.

NEIL: Don't pull that shit, you owe me the truth. Just when it was all coming together out there, you were hot, had dynamite credits—

DAN: Yeah, some credits I had.

NEIL: Three Movies of the Week, in on budget! Okay, so maybe they weren't masterpieces—

DAN: Masterpieces! Neil! Downhill racer loses leg and makes triumphant comeback on single ski? They reran that one on cable last year and I got sick watching it. Physically ill.

NEIL: Everyone takes a little shitwork at first, paying dues.

DAN: It was something *I had done.* My legacy. "Directed by . . ." And worse, Neil, I was actually starting to get just a little bit, oh Jesus, *proud* of that work. You know the feeling. I'm on the way. I'm big time. Even Julia was proud, and why not—we were "making it." Except, what was I making, Neil? Lies about some dingdong world full of good guys and bad guys: "Here we go, folks, turn off your brains once again and watch in a stupor while the villains get punished and the heroes crowned with glory, music, credits; time to wake up." What did every producer say about our infamous screenplay? "Where's the good guy, fellows? You gotta show me who to root for." And what if we *had* found some money—no, to get really wild here, let's say we'd made a moderately successful film we could show the money boys and say, "See, that's what we mean; no heroes, no villains, an entire story celebrating people as they really are." You think they'd have said, "Oh, hey, I see your point, here's money, do more?" Not on your life. They don't want to know, Neil. Make it simple, make it pretty, make it fake, and never mind that the audience comes away, oh yes, happy for an hour or two; but when the glitter fades, what are they left with? A little restlessness . . . frustration, even shame at their own lives that seem so much more complicated and confusing and drab so they have to run back to the movies for another escape, another fix, another lie, until they've totally forgotten how to see and feel and think about their own existence . . . (*Stops.*) Oh, man, listen to me. Rehearsing the defense; day in, day out, rehearsing the defense. I don't know what happened to me out there, Neil. And that's the truth. I wanted it all so badly—

NEIL: Aha!

DAN: Yeah, the whole nine yards. Respect. Power—

NEIL: Money—

DAN: Sure, that too; I'm an American. So why couldn't I fit in? There were good people in the business, they had no problem with it. That's why one day I decided to just stop fighting and fall back in the warm water; do my work, believe the praise, put the dreams behind. It felt so goddamn wonderful to just give in and embrace it all. Went out to celebrate alone. Got blotto. Woke up one week later in the nuthouse.

NEIL: We found you on Sunset. A bench. Guy said you'd been there for three days, sitting.

DAN: I don't remember. Only faces . . . bustle . . . motion. I'd sort of fly out into people's heads, try to get inside and see through their eyes, what made 'em go on, do things. Had to be some purpose under all that bustle. Hope, maybe? Faith in something, themselves, God, the future?

NEIL: What? What'd you see?

DAN: I saw . . . I saw *nothing*. A total void. And for the first time ever in my life I knew what it felt like to be free. Because it doesn't matter, you see. All this striving to make something useful, good, lasting. What's the point. All that's left now is a slow dance to the end of the future.

Thunder. NEIL *looks at the sky.*

NEIL: Okay, okay, he's just talking.

DAN: Ralph says it; eat, fuck, and make merry.

NEIL: Why teach if nothing matters?

DAN: Gotta be keeping busy with this 'n that. I don't know—leftover hope? Old habits die hard.

NEIL: How can you teach what you're afraid to do?

DAN: You'll never understand—

NEIL: Don't you wish. I understand you so well it hurts. You're my other half. You care so much it drives you nuts, you always did; that's what made you important. But you left me out there.

DAN: You're a big boy, Neil, you can take care of yourself.

NEIL: I wasn't made to go it alone. With you I'd have fought till the end, but you just laid down your weapons and ran.

DAN: Whoa, Toomie, don't blame your fucking life on me—

NEIL: No blame. I chose my life. But don't bullshit a dying man with end-of-the-world talk because the world's still here, for you anyway, and what you do is seen: every tree in the forest has eyes, and when one of them falls . . . oh, fuck, Danny, you'd see it right away if you could just step in here with me for a minute and catch

71

one glimpse of the last horizit (*means horizon*) . . . hirr-
rizz . . . hrrr. (*Pause.*) Duh. Da. Daaah (*means
Dan*) . . .

NEIL *looks puzzled by his disobedient mouth,
which moves but makes no sounds.*

DAN: What? Neil? Should I do something? Neil, come on,
buddy, talk to me . . . talk to me.

NEIL, *helpless, shakes his head.*

*   *   *

ADEN *comes forward and speaks.*

ADEN: I think I can honestly say I've never met anyone who
I didn't find, somehow, absolutely fascinating. In fact, I
can't conceive of such a thing as an uninteresting person. Even . . . well, even an insurance salesman from,
say, La Porte, Indiana could come up to me and say,
"Hello there, my name is Bill Smithers and I'm the
most boring person in the world," and I just know I'd
be thinking, "How fascinating! I wonder what makes
him feel he's so boring? I wonder why he chose to tell
me?" Because I'm sure, at certain moments, perhaps
when he's not monitoring his brain too carefully, this
man must have the most incredibly unexpected
thoughts, even perhaps a little *wild*! He might, for example, picture himself riding naked on the back of a
very large giraffe and waving to a crowd of frenzied dis-
ciples clad in a certain kind of peculiar silver uniform.
Or perhaps he sees himself alone on a remote tropical
island with an incredibly beautiful woman. Or an incredibly ugly one. Or perhaps the only person in the
world who has such thoughts is *me*. But I just somehow

doubt that very much. Now don't misunderstand. I'm not saying there aren't people who I find just totally obnoxious . . . and overbearing . . . and rude and even just completely *repellent*. But that doesn't mean they aren't somehow fascinating in their own overbearing and repellent way. I'm sorry, but that's simply how I see things. You may disagree entirely. In fact I hope you do. Because, really, when you think about it, if everyone saw things exactly as I do, well, the world wouldn't be nearly as interesting a place as it is. And that's really all I have to say.

*   *   *

DAN *and* JULIA's *living room*—NEIL *sits on the couch, speaking into the phone.* DAN *sits across the room at a table with a whiskey bottle and two glasses, watching him.* NEIL's *manner is full of simple wonder, like a child wakened into a world of sweet, miraculous objects.*

NEIL (*into the phone*): A zebra! You feeded him crackers? He sneezed them back in your face—oh no! (*To* DAN:) The zoo. (*Into the phone:*) No, sugarpuss, I was talking to a freng . . . feng, in New York. Yes, the place in the picture book with the big tall biddilings . . . billid, *houses.* I am *not* talking funny, you sillyface. Daddy's fine, sugar.

The doorbell rings. DAN *goes to answer, letting in* RALPH *with doctor's bag.*

Yes, I'll talk to Mommy. I miss you too, sugarpuss. (*Pause.*) Hello, Michelle. (*Beat.*) No, we had to come back a little earnily . . . earny. (*Beat.*) I want to stay here. (*Beat.*) Because; better for the big one inside other man. (*Beat.*) I'm sorry, Michelle, sometimes it's a problem with the worms . . . worrmm, *saythings.*

> NEIL *holds the phone away from his ear.* DAN *takes it as* RALPH *opens his bag and fetches out a notebook, instruments, whatever, and prepares to examine* NEIL.

DAN (*into the phone*): It's me, Michelle. (*Beat.*) He had a few seizures. (*Beat.*) There *is* a doctor here. (*Pause.*) I understand, but if he wants to stay— (*Beat.*) She's not here. (*Beat.*) Out, Michelle, I don't know *where*, I'll tell her to call you the minute— (*Beat.*) Yes, I'm aware of the time. (*Pause.*) Michelle, I realize you're upset, but I'll forget you said that . . . Michelle!

> DAN *holds the phone away from his ear, gestures to* NEIL, *who waves "no."* DAN *hangs up the phone and punches on the anwering machine.*

RALPH: Is he on any medication?

DAN (*produces pills*): Doctor down south gave us these.

RALPH (*checks the bottle*): Good as any. Well, chum, looks like time for the hospital. There's a bed available at Columbia Presbyterian—I've checked.

DAN: Should I pack his things?

NEIL: Don't go.

DAN: I'm right in there. (*Exits.*)

RALPH (*checks* NEIL*'s eyes*): Any dizziness? Headaches? Loss of balance?

NEIL: Some.

RALPH: Dan said you asked for poison. Is that true?

NEIL (*pause*): Yes.

RALPH: Do you still want it?

NEIL (*beat*): You'll get me?

RALPH: There're some pretty rough times ahead.

NEIL (*pause*): Don't want poison. No.

RALPH: Good lad. Of course I'd not give it to you. It's against the rules for one thing. Just curious. Why give death an easy victory, it always wins in the end. But the fight, you see, that's what counts. Even when it's hopeless. No, especially then; life for life's sake. Shouldn't need any more reason than that. (*The exam is over.*) So, how does it feel to be no longer among the entirely quick and not yet with the entirely dead?

NEIL (*smiles*) Weird.

RALPH: Yes. Welcome to exile.

NEIL: Why am I . . . dine?

RALPH (*pause*): By the by, and for God sake don't tell Aden, he'd have me guts for garters, but if you still feel up for a bit of the other, I know a very exotic creature I could slip past the nurses. She specializes in hospitals. Never heard the like till I met her. Marvellous thing about this country, the sheer variety. Cheers!

> NEIL *erupts with laughter as* RALPH *drinks*
> *from the whiskey bottle. Both are laughing.*
> DAN *reenters, bag in hand.*

DAN: Did I miss something?

RALPH: Just discussing ways to extend life.

DAN: Should I call an ambulance?

RALPH: Taxi's cheaper. You can still stumble about, yes?

> NEIL *nods. The phone rings. The machine*
> *clicks on as* JULIA *rushes in through the front*
> *door to answer. She stops, face flushed.*

JULIA: What are you all doing here?

> TOM *enters with champagne bottle.*

DAN: Ah, Tom! How nice to see you here. At this hour.

TOM (*lifts the bottle*): We were celebrating. Julia didn't get the job.

RALPH (*beat*): Dear me, and to think of all the times I tried to get her into bed. You have no taste, Julia.

JULIA: Why is everybody back?

DAN: We're taking Neil to the hospital, dear. He hasn't been feeling well. We hope it's nothing serious.

NEIL: I'm fine. No problem.

TOM (*pause*): I guess I ought to be hitting the trail. Never mind, Julia, they made a big mistake, in my humble opinion—

DAN: Tom, just get the hell out of here.

JULIA: Dan!

DAN: *What*, Julia!

TOM (*to* DAN): You know something? You're a damn fool. If I had a woman like your wife, I'd worship the ground she walked on. I'd throw rose petals in her path. I'd bring her breakfast in bed. I'd . . . I'd hire a gypsy violin to play while we dined at home together alone, just the two of us. God, I'm so drunk. I lost my job, you see. Sorry, Julia, I meant not to say that, you've had enough bad news for one day. And anyway, what's the big deal? They made it sound like the end of the world, but I was just laughing inside. I mean, there're so many important things to be done. Why didn't they tell us in school how good life could be? (*Beat.*) Good night, Julia. (*Exits.*)

RALPH (*pause*): My, my, hidden depths.

DAN: Would you like to come to the hospital with us, darling?

NEIL (*looks at* DAN, *then* JULIA): Tomorrow. Visit when I'm comfortable. I'm talking really well.

JULIA: Can we bring you anything?

NEIL (*thinks*): Hospital food. (*Gets an idea.*) Cheeseburger! Slice of raw onion—

JULIA: Mustard, tomato, relish . . . I remember.

NEIL (*to* JULIA): You look so . . . like you used to.

> NEIL *hugs* JULIA, *takes up his bag, staggers slightly, rights himself.*

RALPH (*helping*): Steady on . . .

NEIL (*with deliberate walk*): Left foot. Right foot. Left foot. Windup toys.

RALPH: I'll call when he's settled in.

> RALPH *and* NEIL *exit, followed by* DAN *carrying* NEIL's *bag.*

JULIA (*alone*): Good-bye, Neil.

DAN (*pause; reenters*): Sorry to bust up a fun evening.

JULIA: You didn't make your film.

DAN: Technical difficulties.

JULIA: Oh well, some other time.

DAN: *What* did you say?

JULIA: Some other time. You'll make your film some other time. I'll get a job some other time. Things will all work out some other time. Or they won't. Whatever.

DAN: You're drunk.

JULIA: Oh if only. You're back so soon. I thought I'd have more time.

DAN: For what?

JULIA: To think it through. To be sure. In the morning— we'll talk then. I want it to come out the right way.

DAN: More surprises? And here I was ready to settle for my wife coming home drunk at two in the morning with her lover while my best friend is dying.

JULIA: Dying, yes. No more chance you'll pick up the phone one day, "Neil, it's me, the time of healing is over, we're on our way, rent us a place, let's try it again." And our life will suddenly make sense again.

DAN: You're not saying you actually thought that would happen.

JULIA: That's Julia for you; never knows when to give up.

DAN: What's going on here?

JULIA: I make a very nice impression. But I don't seem qualified for anything. If it's not too personal, may we ask exactly what you've been up to all these years? That was my interview.

DAN: I'm sorry, Julia. I am.

JULIA: Well, Mr. Ross, I used to help my husband, that is until he stopped doing what I was so good at helping him with. I know, I know, I should have gotten on with my own career but you see, working together was so very much a part of our life . . . (*Stops.*)

DAN: Julia, just tell me what this is all about.

JULIA: I'm a dilettante. Neil is dying. There are no miracles; it's all just the way you said. So with all this incredible clarity of vision, I'd like to know what you see when you look at yourself?

DAN: This feels dangerous.

JULIA: What am I supposed to make of a man who said that without directing, his life had no purpose.

DAN: That was a long time ago.

JULIA: Then what are you now, Danny. *What are you now?*

DAN: Go on.

JULIA: Well don't you think you've become just a little bit . . . (*Stops.*)

DAN: Yes?

JULIA: Oh, lordy, I *am* drunk.

DAN: Tell me, Julia, what do you think I've become.

JULIA: This isn't what I meant to talk about—

DAN: Say it, god damn it, just say it.

JULIA: Funny, I always wanted to be with someone better than me. Why is that?

DAN: Say it, say it, say it: a little disappointing, a little weak, a fraud, a coward, all of the above!

JULIA: YEEESSS! (*Sudden embrace.*) Yes, Dan, I'm sorry, but yes. We came to each other with promises about who we were, and you broke yours and it's not fair, it's just not fair.

DAN (*moves away*): Eureka! I wondered when you'd open your eyes and see it. I expected trumpets and thunder to mark the revelation. Instead . . . silence. Plink. It feels like nothing at all. It feels like the truth.

JULIA: About both of us. We tiptoe around this apartment terrified of any reference to that dread subject of subjects: The Life They Once Had.

DAN: To whom do we owe this great awakening—Tom?

JULIA: There was this student, you see—

DAN: Christ, not that again.

JULIA : But you were right. When you're stuck, try anything—plant a bomb, light the fuse, ka-boom, see where the pieces fall. (*Beat.*) I need time on my own.

DAN: Yes, I thought that was coming. Good to have it in plain English. Is this for a while . . . or for more than a while?

JULIA: I'm not sure yet.

DAN: Is there a schedule? Like, when you were planning to vacate the premises. I presume you'll be moving in with Tom.

JULIA: No.

DAN: Oh dear, the best man didn't win.

JULIA: Poor Tom. He has no idea what he's in for.

DAN: Tom will be fine, darling. You know, saving the world and all.

JULIA: Yes, Danny, exactly. Maybe he looks a little foolish, but at least he believes he can make a difference. The way *we* used to believe. No, *you*; it was always *your* passion, *your* faith. I thought it was only people like you who could know that excitement. People with a gift. It's not true. Look at Tom. He's no different from me, nothing special, but he's found a way to believe in something and it makes him alive. That's what I want to feel. Not through you, not through anyone else: *my own faith*. It's amazing what's been going through my head these past few days—all these plans, all these ideas. It's terrible, Danny, but I feel so . . . happy!

DAN: How nice. Sorry I can't work up a little more enthusiasm—it's the timing, you know. But, hell, why be a killjoy, life goes on, let's open the champagne, drink a toast to . . . what? Keeping in touch? Growing as individuals? To a fair division of the video cassettes? Nice touch, to round off our waning years together with a gift from this man who inspired my wife to such lofty new purpose. A toast to Tom. Get the glasses—

JULIA: Danny . . .

DAN (*finally breaks*): Don't leave me, Julia. You're the only one left who knows what I can be. The whole world is dying with Neil, and afterwards there'll be nothing left but regrets and excuses and all that time to fill. Don't make it cost any more, please, God, Julia, don't leave me now.

JULIA *stands helpless, torn.*

*   *   *

NEIL *steps forward in a white hospital gown and speaks clearly, simply.*

NEIL: Towards the end, the very end, when I couldn't speak and my eyesight was failing, even then there were moments of such luminous clarity. Memories. Colors. Sensations. Small islands in the sea of pain worth struggling to reach. God knows where they came from. Ah yes, God! I saw him. Well, something I took to be *His glory*: a kind of limitless whiteness surrounding me. I thought to myself, "That's Him, that's the Big Guy. How typical, even when I'm rattling at the gates he plays all coy and anonymous." I shouted questions into the whiteness. "Hey, God, this life of mine, did I choose how it went or was it all Thy Plan?" Silence. "Was it a sick joke, pulling the rug from under me so young, or was it a gesture wherein to read some larger meaning?" Silence. "If you were driving all along, why torment me with the illusion that every wrong turn was my own doing?" Silence. No, a voice sometimes: Danny's voice. I'd hear it through the white fog. He was there beside my bed for . . . must have been weeks, talking the whole time. Talking. I knew what he was up to. Trying to hold my attention, as if his stories had the power to spin out a thread of life for me to cling to. I loved him for that. Made little noises so he'd think he was getting through. You have to humor the living, they don't have it easy. All those hours and days and years to fill with motion. Fuck it, I'd had my turn. I'd find out soon enough if I'd won my wings. If, indeed, that's what's waiting. Who knows. Nice to pass on into the bosom of such certainty.

* * *

Hospital—NEIL *in bed, torso raised slightly.* NURSE *changes drip.* MICHELLE-MARIE *stands in the doorway with a bag of take-out*

food. DAN *is asleep in a chair.* MICHELLE-
MARIE *moves into the room.*

MICHELLE-MARIE (*whispers*): Danny?

DAN (*jolts awake*): Neil!

MICHELLE-MARIE: He's right here.

DAN: Any change?

NURSE: Ten o'clock and all's well. If you need anything,
hoot and holler. I have to check the floor. (*Exits.*)

DAN: How you holding up?

MICHELLE-MARIE: It's hell without the pills. Everything
looks so damn . . . solid, you know what I mean? Hey,
you were in my dream last night. You, me, and Neil.
After a war. We were the last people on earth and we
had to start a whole new human race.

DAN: And?

MICHELLE-MARIE: That's it. We just stood around in this
kind of rubble waiting for someone to make the first
move. Pretty dumb, huh? (*Beat.*) I'm real sorry about
you and Julia.

DAN: We just decided to live apart for a while.

MICHELLE-MARIE: That's not what she told *me*. (*Stops.*)
Shoot, me and my big mouth.

DAN: We need a little time on our own. That's how you stay
together in New York. Take the sofa in the lounge, I'll
be all right.

MICHELLE-MARIE: I wish I knew what it was between you
guys. I wish I knew what that felt like. Extra cheeseburger? (DAN *indicates no.*) Do you like kids?

DAN: Why?

MICHELLE-MARIE: Case you're wrong about Julia, we'll both be in the market pretty soon. No way, huh? Just a thought.

> MICHELLE-MARIE *kisses* NEIL *on the forehead and starts out.* DAN *takes her hands in a gesture of support. She exits.*

DAN: Hey, old buddy, anyone home? (NEIL *makes noise.*) "Then what happened?" Funny you should ask. Shit, Toomie, I'm running out of stories here. Have to start my whole life again from the beginning. Bore you to death, huh? (NEIL *makes noise.*) That a smile? How 'bout this for a yuk—your favorite Wandering Jew offers up his life for confession to a half-dead fallen Catholic. (*Beat.*) I dozed off just before, dreamed you were already . . . (*Stops.* NEIL *makes noise.*) But your eyes . . . they wouldn't close. (*Pause.*) Neil, forgive me. For a moment, when I learned you were dying, I felt such relief . . . to be rid of you and your blind fucking faith in me. How did I ever think I could make myself stop caring. Forgive me, Neil. Please God, let him hear that. (NEIL *makes noise.*) Hey, guess what, the "horrible film" guy called. Yeah, wants to talk about a project, ho-ho. Why don't you stop this bullshit dying act and come with me. You could always hustle better than me. I figured out exactly what I'm gonna hit him with—you'll love this . . . (*Pause.*) Neil? Neil . . . you there? Hey, Toomie?

> DAN *checks* NEIL. NEIL *is dead.* DAN *looks at the ceiling for a moment, then back at* NEIL.

84

I'll miss you.

*　　*　　*

*Secluded area near film set—*DAN *paces in a heavy coat, smoking, deep in thought.* LAUREL *rushes in with head-phone walkie-talkie.*

LAUREL: Dan, everyone's looking for you—what are you doing back here? (*Into the walkie-talkie.*) Lester, I found him, he's behind the honey wagon. (*To* DAN.) Do you want any extras in the restaurant setup?

DAN: Yeah, fill the tables; I'll give 'em stuff to do.

LAUREL: But the next shot's a close-up. We're right in tight on Renata's face—

DAN: She can't play the scene without people around— you'll see. Just put everyone at the tables, Laurel. Watch and learn. (*Pause.*) What?

LAUREL: I want to thank you for getting me this job.

DAN: Don't thank me, just do it well. Now go.

AVRAM (*enters, agitated*): Daniel, why are you back here. The lights are in position and we all wait.

DAN: Just thinking through the sequence, Avram; with you in a minute.

AVRAM: This thinking you do at night—not on my time when it cost many thousands of dollars each hour; and why a close-up when I pay so many extras to be here today?

DAN: Because, Avram, according to our contract I can't make a real film for you until I've made this piece of shit for you first, but there's a very slight chance I can make even this piece of shit look less like a piece of shit than

85

the piece of shit it really is if you'll let me do it my way, which means primarily get the fuck off my back.

AVRAM: Not good, Daniel. I make you here on trial only. I have other ovens in the fire, you know.

DAN: When the hell are you going to learn to speak English.

AVRAM (*enormous pleasure*): It goes well, yes?

DAN: It just might if you'll piss off and let me work.

AVRAM: I never misjudge a man! (*To* LAUREL.) You! Come. (*Exits.*)

LAUREL: My name is Laurel, not You Come. (*Exits, speaking into walkie-talkie.*) He wants the tables filled—that's what he said—and you better move the equipment vans . . .

> DAN *alone, speaks to us.*

DAN: Pain in the ass, Avram. Doesn't know the first thing about . . . (*Stops, smiles.*) He's okay. Crazy too. Who else'd take such a chance. No one has the slightest idea how scared I am. Feel like I'm faking it half the time. But you go on. For whatever reason. For Neil, maybe. For some guy in Haifa. China. Mars. *For other people.* You never know who you might touch one day . . . and ignite. Small fact: Neil's gone. Another small fact, so small in the midst of everything, but there you are: I'm working again. And it feels . . . *right.*

> DAN *exits.*